A Brief Introduction to Hinduism

A Brief Introduction to Hinduism

Religion, Philosophy, and Ways of Liberation

A. L. Herman

Westview Press
BOULDER • SAN FRANCISCO • OXFORD

Published in 1991 in the United States of America by Westview Press, Inc., 5500 Central Avenue, Boulder, Colorado 80301, and in the United Kingdom by Westview Press, 36 Lonsdale Road, Summertown, Oxford OX2 7EW

Library of Congress Cataloging-in-Publication Data
Herman, A. L.
A brief introduction to Hinduism : religion, philosophy, and ways of liberation / A. L. Herman.
p. cm.
Includes bibliographical references and index.
ISBN 0-8133-8109-6. — ISBN 0-8133-8110-X (pbk.)
1. Hinduism—Doctrines—Introductions. 2. Hinduism—Doctrines—History. 3. Philosophy, Hindu—History. 4. Hinduism—History. 5. Hindus—History—20th century. 6. Hindus—Case studies. I. Title.
BL1212.72.H47 1991
294.5—dc20 90-25262
CIP

Printed and bound in the United States of America

The paper used in this publication meets the requirements of the American National Standard for Permanence of Paper for Printed Library Materials Z39.48-1984.

10 9 8

For Beth
and Arthur

Contents

Tables and Figures

Tables

Figures

Preface

One of the assumptions of this book is that religions and philosophies exist primarily to solve human problems. Another assumption is that religions and philosophies survive by coping successfully with human problems. From these assumptions three testable consequences follow: First, religious and philosophic activities ought to reflect a problem-*identifying* purpose; second, religious and philosophic activities ought to reflect a problem-*solving* purpose; third, one fruitful way of understanding a religion or a philosophy would be to discover what problems they are trying to solve and how they go about solving them. Our task in this brief book will be to understand Hinduism in precisely these terms, namely, by empirically discovering the problems that it faces and the solutions that it offers to those problems. In carrying out this task the book will focus of necessity on texts and thought rather than on ritual and worship.

In Chapter 1 we shall examine three extremely different Hindu problem solvers of the twentieth century, namely, Mohandas Gandhi, Ramana Maharshi, and A. C. Bhaktivedanta. But why these three? Why not three other Hindus, with more fame at home and with greater worldwide recognition abroad, authors, educators, artists, Nobel laureates, scientists, and military leaders? To see Hinduism as a problem-identifying and problem-solving discipline it is necessary to see Hindu problem solvers in religious and philosophic action. And the Hindus that were chosen for that purpose not only had to be committed problem solvers but, in addition, had to satisfy three other conditions for inclusion here. First, they had to be living in the twentieth century and be recognized for making a continuing impact on their times and on their followers or disciples; second, each had to reflect one of the three major religious traditions or religious ways within Hinduism, namely, the way of selfless action, the way of mystical absorption, and the way of worshipful devotion; third, and for reasons that will be apparent shortly, each had to have composed a critical commentary on the one text that more than any other epitomizes Hinduism--the *Bhagavad Gītā*. In addition, the choice of these three Hindus reflects an added bonus that will become more obvious as our analysis of Hindus and Hinduism proceeds. These three men represent the three major vocational (or "caste") levels of traditional Indian society: Gandhi, from the west, was a politician, a statesman, and represented by his actions the traditional ruling or princely class of ancient India (even though he was not a kṣatriya by birth); Maharshi, from the south, was a religious mystic and represented by his actions the traditional priestly class of ancient India (he was a brahmin by birth); Bhaktivedanta, from the east, was a worshipful devotee of Lord Kṛṣṇa and represented by his actions the traditional merchant class of ancient India (he was a vaiṣya by birth). These three men represent Hinduism in the twentieth century--men whose religious and philosophic views, as we shall see, were so different from one another.

Which brings me to the central question that shall be raised with respect to those religious and philosophic views: How could these three men offer such diverse solutions to the religious and philosophic problems of Hinduism, solutions that must seem so patently opposed to one another, and still be called "Hindus"? The answer to this question not only will lead us into the religious and philosophic views of these three modern thinkers, but it also will plunge us into the depths of the Hindu religious and philosophic system itself.

In Chapter 2 we look to the root of those three ancient traditions of Hinduism: first, in the archaeological remains of the Indus Valley civilization (2500-1800 B.C.E.); second, to the sacred compositions, called the *Vedas,* of the Āryan invaders (1500-900 B.C.E.) who displaced that civilization; and, third, to the secret teachings of the *Upaniṣads* (800-200 B.C.E.) that attempted to offer a new and revolutionary alternative to the *Vedas.* Each of our modern Hindu problem solvers--Gandhi, Maharshi, and Bhaktivedanta--was influenced in quite different ways by those remains and by the *Vedas* and *Upaniṣads,* and we shall try to see what those various influences were.

In Chapter 3 we turn from these three ancient traditions of Hinduism to the attempt that was made at synthesizing the Indus and pre-Vedic tradition, the Vedic tradition, and the Upaniṣadic tradition. That synthesis is carried out in what has become the most popular and universally recognized text of Hinduism--the *Bhagavad Gītā* (ca. 200 B.C.E.). Each of our modern sages, Gandhi, Maharshi, and Bhaktivedanta, gave quite different interpretations of this most powerful and influential text, and we shall be at some pains to note those differences in our discussion.

In the fourth and final chapter we shall analyze and summarize the results of our investigations into the problem-identifying and problem-solving ways of Gandhi, Maharshi, and Bhaktivedanta, of the ancient traditions found in the Indus Valley civilization, the *Vedas,* and the *Upaniṣads,* and of the *Bhagavad Gītā.* Following this analysis and summary we should then be able, first, to understand what Hinduism is as a result of understanding the three problem-identifying and problem-solving traditions in it as represented by Gandhi, Maharshi, and Bhaktivedanta, and, second, to answer the question with which the first chapter begins: How could these three men hold views that seem so opposed to one another and still be called Hindus? The history of Hinduism as well as the lives of these three Hindus are the best empirical evidence that we have for the three quite powerful and distinguishable traditions in Hinduism.

A. L. Herman

Acknowledgments

For permission to reprint copyrighted material in excess of fair use I would like to thank the following:

Excerpts from A. C. Bhaktivedanta Swami Prabhupada, *Bhagavad-gītā As It Is*, Complete Edition (London: Collier-Macmillan Ltd., 1972) reprinted by permission of Bhaktivedanta Book Trust International.

The picture of His Divine Grace A. C. Bhaktivedanta is taken from *Back to Godhead, The Magazine of the Hare Krishna Movement*, Vol. 19, No. 4, April 1984. Reprinted by permission.

Excerpts from Mahadev Desai, *The Gita According to Gandhi* (Ahmedabad: Navajivan Publishing House, 1946). Reprinted by permission.

The picture "At the Spinning Wheel," which appears in Appendix A, is from M. K. Gandhi, *An Autobiography or The Story of My Experiments with Truth*, translated from the original Gujarati by Mahadev Desai (Ahmedabad: Navajivan Publishing House, 1948) opposite p. 609. Reprinted by permission.

The photographs of the Indus Valley sculptures and seals are taken from Volumes I and III of Sir John Marshall et al., *Mohenjodaro and the Indus Civilization*, 3 Volumes (London: Arthur Probsthain, 1931) and appear through the permission of the publisher and the Archeological Survey of India, Government of India.

The photographs of Ramana Maharshi and the spoken words quoted from *The Collected Works of Ramana Maharshi* and *Maharshi's Gospel* are reprinted here with the very kind permission of Sri Ramanasramam, Tiruvannamalai.

Excerpts from T.M.P. Mahadevan, *Ramana Maharshi, The Sage of Arunacala* (London: George Allen & Unwin, Ltd., 1977). Reprinted by permission.

Excerpts from Wendy Doniger O'Flaherty, *Hindu Myths: A Sourcebook Translated from the Sanskrit* (Baltimore: Penguin Classics, 1975), copyright (c) Wendy Doniger O'Flaherty. Reprinted by permission.

A number of people have given of their time, talents, and energy to the completion of this work: Carolee Cote, as usual, typed, word-processed, and photocopied her way through the multiple versions and revisions of this book; Barbara Herman, as usual, read and reread the entire manuscript in varying stages of its development, all the while offering her transcendentally sound advice, "Cut it!"; my eloquent and highly perceptive Hindological colleagues, Wendy Doniger of the University of Chicago and Harold Coward of the University of Calgary, as well as my perspicacious editor, Spencer Carr, and his compassionate staff of Jeanne Campbell, Stephen Haenel, and Marykay Scott at Westview Press, have all made extraordinary comments and criticisms toward the improvement of the manuscript, and in the process they have saved it and me from flagrant errors and conspicuous embarrassment; and, finally, my Indological colleagues, Gary Alexander, John Bailiff, Eliot Deutsch, Frank J. Hoffman, David J. Kalupahana, John M. Koller, Bimal K. Matilal, Thomas Overholt, S. S. Rama Rao Pappu, and Karl H. Potter, have all been pressed into service at one time or another to criticize and to comment on aspects of both this work and its author.

The errors that this book contains are entirely my own. Whatever merit the work possesses is due entirely to the collective kindness, wit, and attention of all of the above extremely generous persons.

A. L. H.

The Pronunciation of Sanskrit Terms

Sanskrit is written in an ancient and elegant script called *devanāgarī.* For those who do not read devanāgarī this script is transliterated into English and pronounced according to the following phonetic rules of Sanskrit:

The vowels with macrons, or lines, over them, *ā, ī, ū,* are long vowels and are pronounced as in *father, machine,* and *rude*. The same vowels without macrons are short vowels and equivalent in sound to the vowels in *but, tin,* and *full*. Vowel *ṛ* is sounded as in rill and is lightly trilled. The vowels *e, ai, o, and au* are considered long and are pronounced as in *gray, aisle, open,* and *cow*.

All consonants with *h* after them are aspirated consonants and the breath should be slightly released when pronouncing them. Thus *kh, gh, ch, jh, ph,* and so on sound like *rockhouse, doghouse, churchhouse, fudgehouse,* and *tophouse,* respectively. Other consonants that one must watch out for are *c* as in *cheese; ś* and *ṣ* both as in *ship; s* as in *sip;* and *jñ* as in *gyāna*.

Sanskrit words are stress-accented according to the following simple formulas:

1. Words of two syllables are accented on the first syllable: Veda, Gītā, dharma.

2. Words of more than two syllables, where the penult (second syllable from the end) is either long (i.e., has a long vowel or diphthong, for example, *ā, ī, ū, e, o, au, or ai*) or has a short vowel followed by two or more consonants (and where *kh, gh, th, ph,* and *bh* count as one consonant), are accented on the penult: Hīnayāna, Subhadra, Abhidharma.

3. Words of more than two syllables where the penult is short and not followed by two consonants, as above, are accented on the antepenult (third syllable from the end): Bṛhadāraṇyaka, Upaniṣad, Bhagavan.

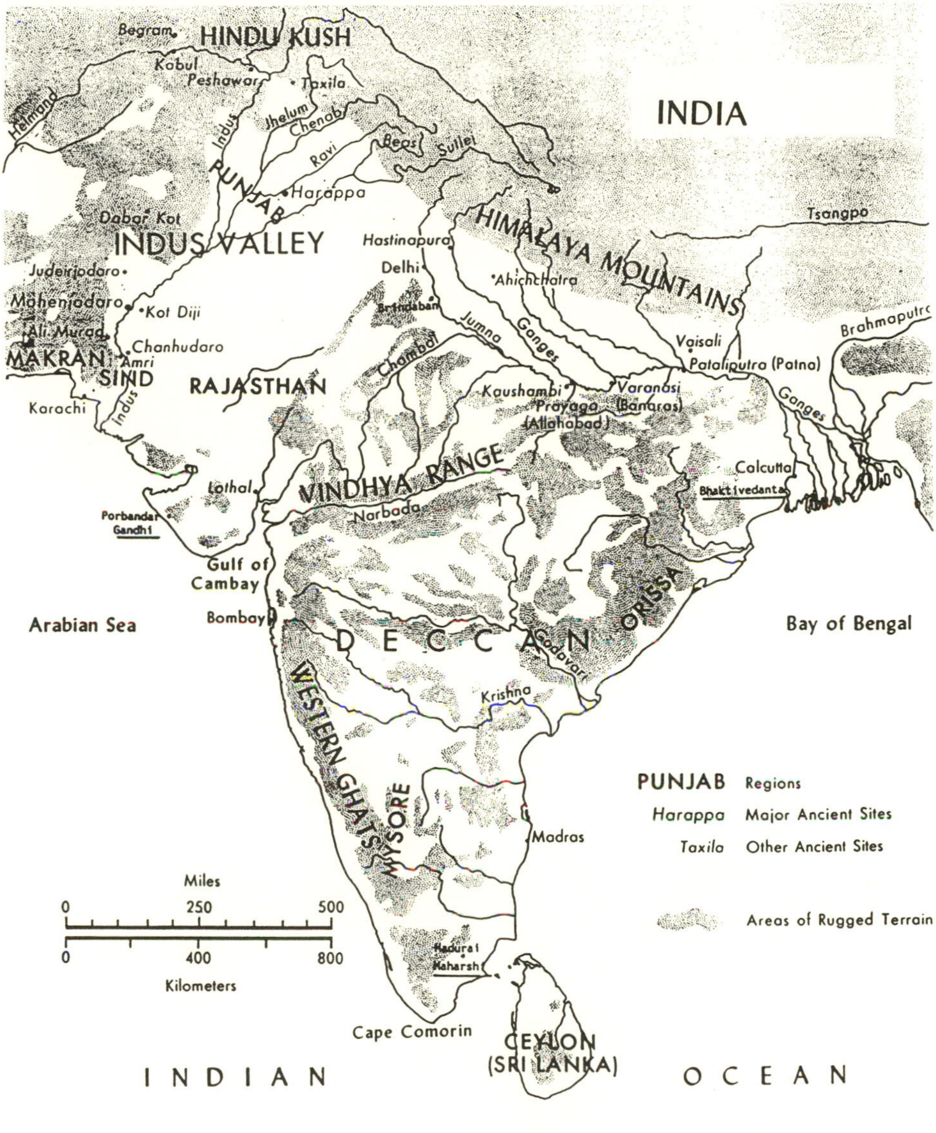

Begram
HINDU KUSH
Kabul
Peshawar
Taxila
Helmand
INDIA
Indus
Jhelum
Chenab
Ravi
Beas
Sutlej
PUNJAB
Harappa
Dabar Kot
INDUS VALLEY
Hastinapura
Delhi
HIMALAYA MOUNTAINS
Tsangpo
Judeirjodaro
Mohenjodaro
Kot Diji
Ali Murad
Chanhudaro
Amri
MAKRAN
SIND
Karachi
RAJASTHAN
Ahichchatra
Jumna
Ganges
Chambal
Vaisali
Pataliputra (Patna)
Brahmaputra
Kaushambi
Varanasi
(Banaras)
Prayaga
(Allahabad)
VINDHYA RANGE
Calcutta
Bhaktivedanta
Lothal
Porbandar
Gandhi
Narbada
Gulf of Cambay
ORISSA
Arabian Sea
Bombay
DECCAN
Godavari
Bay of Bengal
WESTERN GHATS
Krishna
MYSORE
Madras
PUNJAB Regions
Harappa Major Ancient Sites
Taxila Other Ancient Sites
Areas of Rugged Terrain
Miles
0
250
500
0
400
800
Kilometers
Maharshi
Cape Comorin
CEYLON
(SRI LANKA)
INDIAN
OCEAN

Shine on us with thy radiant light,
    Oh Uṣas, daughter of the sky.
Bring to us great store of high felicity,
    and beam down now on our solemn
    rites.

Ṛg Veda I. 48. 9

From the unreal lead me to the real.
From darkness lead me to light.
From death lead me to immortality.

Bṛhadāraṇyaka Upaniṣad I. 3 28

You are truly my beloved.... Merge your
    mind with Me, be my devotee,
    sacrifice to Me, love Me and you
    shall surely come to Me.... Seek
    refuge in Me alone and I shall
    give you liberation from all sins.

Bhagavad Gītā XVIII. 64-66

1

Three Modern Sages: Mohandas Gandhi, Ramana Maharshi, and A. C. Bhaktivedanta

Three great men have emerged from the turmoil and tangle of modern India to challenge the imaginations and philosophies of 20th century men and women. All three of these men were Hindus and yet they espoused philosophies that seem, in a sense, strongly opposed to one another. The three men who represent these opposed Hindu views are Mohandas Gandhi, Ramana Maharshi, and A. C. Bhaktivedanta.* Each man exemplified one of the three major ancient philosophic traditions of Indian thought and, as a consequence, each man gave to modern India and to the world three quite distinct techniques for solving human problems. This chapter is about these men and their traditions, and the influence of their traditions in solving human problems.

Mohandas Karamchand Gandhi (1869-1948)

Mohandas Karamchand Gandhi was born in 1869 in Porbandar, a city halfway between Bombay and the mouth of the Indus River, on India's Western coast. He came from the vaiśya class, that is the merchant class of the Indian social system, though both his father and grandfather had been prime ministers in the governments of local

*Photographs of Gandhi, Maharshi, and Bhaktivedanta will be found in Appendix A.

princely states. In his famous *Autobiography*, which he subtitled *The Story of My Experiments With Truth*, Gandhi tells of his early life and marriage in India and also of his adventures as a student in London where he went for study at the age of 18 and from which he obtained his degree in law three years later. He also tells of his early life in South Africa where he practiced law, and of his later life in India where he had his most popular success as both a political and a spiritual leader of millions of his compatriots.

But it was Gandhi's experiences in South Africa that shaped him for his later work of reform and active resistance against the British occupation of India. And it was these early experiences in South Africa, applied subsequently in India, that were to help to lead to the eventual freedom of his country from the British in 1947.

As he, himself, tells the story, after he had returned to India from London in 1891, and after two years of unsuccessful law practice in India, he accepted an invitation from some overseas Indians in South Africa to represent their company in certain legal disputes. Totally unprepared for the prejudice and hatred present in South Africa, Gandhi arrived in that country in 1893 with his new degree and his new English clothes looking very much the British gentleman that he thought he had become. In attempting to ride in a first-class railway compartment, for which he held a first-class ticket, he was, because of his dark skin, thrown off the train when a white man complained to the conductor. On the same journey he was beaten for refusing to ride in a coolie's place on a coach. Gandhi was to learn the hard way about racial prejudice in South Africa.

He spent nearly 20 years in that country with his wife and growing family, during which time both he and the unjust laws that he fought slowly changed. He gave up his English clothes and aristocratic ways in exchange for simple Indian peasant dress, and he disciplined himself after the manner of the traditional Indian *sannyāsi* or holy man with prayer, fasting and an increasingly ascetic existence. During this time he developed his philosophy of life and his philosophy of political and social action which may be summed up in one descriptive word: *satyagraha*.

Satyagraha

The practice of satyagraha was first used successfully by Gandhi in South Africa. And it was to become the most potent weapon used by the Gandhians against the British in India, from its first employment in Bihar in 1917 until 1947, when independence was finally granted.

Satyagraha, as Gandhi was to demonstrate time and again, is composed of four essential elements. First, civil disobedience must be offered to unjust laws. The Gandhians believe that if the law injures human dignity or causes human suffering then one must choose to disobey the law by intentionally courting ridicule, jail, physical injury, imprisonment, or even death. The *satyagrahi,* as the Gandhian follower of satyagraha came to be called, must be prepared for the physical, the legal, and the moral consequences of his or her act of civil disobedience. Civil disobedience to unjust laws is important because it attracts and marshals public attention, that is, the attention of those who support the unjust law, of those who are against it, as well as the attention of those who are indifferent because they never thought about it before. And such attention is necessary in order to change opinions.

Second, the disobedience must be carried out in an attitude of nonviolence and love. The satyagrahis, after fasting and prayer, must conduct themselves in a morally exemplary manner so as not to injure those who would attempt to oppose their disobedience.

Third, Gandhi exhorted his satyagrahis to look upon the act of disobedience as an offering of their bodies, souls, and lives to God. Thus an element of what we shall later refer to as *bhakti yoga,* the way of loving devotion to God, enters into satyagraha. The offering of disobedience becomes a sacrifice, a spiritual act, a religious rite within a social or political environment where the results or fruits of the act, through what we shall later refer to as *karma yoga,* are unselfishly renounced by the satyagrahi.

The fourth and final element of satyagraha followed hard upon the second and third. Gandhi thought, since people were more important than laws and institutions, that the aim of satyagraha should be to change the hearts and minds of the oppressor and the opponent: Only when those who had previously supported and defended the unjust law had been converted could one say that satyagraha had been successful.

Satyagraha, therefore, is simple but intentional disobedience to unjust laws, carried out with an attitude of love, courage, selflessness, and nonviolence as a religious sacrifice to God who, Gandhi believed, would then bless and aid such an undertaking. All of this is done for the sole purpose, not of defeating and triumphantly subduing one's opponent, but of converting or changing him or her. As Gandhi wisely saw, when one *defeats* an opponent in a struggle, one merely sows the seeds of hatred and dissension for future struggles. These four elements of satyagraha were to become the essential ingredients of Gandhi's later prescription for liberation that he used in solving the problems of human existence.

The Great Salt March

One of the most spectacular uses of satyagraha took place in India in 1930. The British government in India, in order to operate the machinery of the state, collected taxes in the usual ways. In particular, the Crown had put a tax on salt which it then proceeded to manufacture. To protect its monopoly, the legislation that put the Salt Act into existence provided stiff penalties for anyone who bootlegged salt or made it illegally. Gandhi felt that the law was unjust. In a letter to the Viceroy, Lord Irwin, the British Crown's representative in New Delhi, dated March 2, 1930, and sent only nine days before his satyagraha against the Salt Act was to begin, Gandhi explained his position and his intention. The letter, addressed to his "Dear Friend," was not only an attempt to get the Viceroy to change the legislation that put an unfair burden on the poverty-driven masses of the country, for whom salt was a necessity of life, but it was also an attempt to convert the Viceroy and to get him to see the error of the very presence of himself and of the British in India. In this extraordinary letter Gandhi went on to inform the Viceroy what he intended to do should the Viceroy fail to respond to his letter: He intended satyagraha. The Viceroy dictated a rude and indifferent reply to Gandhi. The way was now open for the most dramatic act of civil disobedience against the British since the Boston Tea Party of 1773.

On March 12 Gandhi, together with seventy-eight dedicated followers, set out from his *ashram,* or communal retreat, near Ahmedabad, a city north of Bombay, to walk 241 miles in twenty-four days to the sea at Dandi in order to make salt in defiance of the law. Gandhi explained to the crowds of people that they met along the way, "We are marching in the name of God." Wherever he stopped thousands gathered, and Gandhi urged them to give up alcohol and drugs, to abandon child marriage, an ancient custom that Gandhi fought with particular vehemence, and to live virtuously and cleanly. Finally, he exhorted them to join with him in breaking the Salt Law.

He was sixty-one years old at the time and he endured the long march with no visible discomfort, while those younger and seemingly more robust were forced to ride part of the way by cart or even to drop out. The people threw flowers and spread leaves before the satyagrahis as they walked. When finally they arrived at Dandi on April 5, 1930, the band had grown from the original few to tens of thousands.

On April 6th, at 8:00 in the morning, Gandhi walked into the sea, picked up some spume salt from a frothy, foaming wave and returned to the shore. He had broken the law. The pinch of salt, the simplest act imaginable, following a long and dramatic march caught the imagination of the world. The act was a signal to the people of India. Those who accompanied Gandhi waded into the sea to make salt, while up and down the coast of the Arabian Sea entire villages sought to catch the water in their pans and to make salt. And thousands were arrested.

Suddenly, across the country, contraband salt was sold openly while thousands of Indians intentionally and nonviolently broke the law. In Bombay, salt was made on the roof of the Congress Party headquarters. A crowd of over 50,000 gathered, and hundreds were tied and handcuffed and led off to jail. In Ahmedabad over 10,000 people received illegal salt in the first week following the Dandi satyagraha. Jawaharlal Nehru, the leader of the Congress and later the first prime minister of the Republic of India, and still later the father and the grandfather of two future prime ministers of India, was arrested in Allahabad for violating the Salt Law.

The salt satyagraha was also a signal for more nonviolent disobedience to the British presence in India. The people were urged to boycott the British where it would hurt them the most: The pocketbook. The result was a nationwide campaign against all British imports, but especially textiles. Indians began wearing homespun clothing. The spinning wheel, which today appears at the center of the Indian flag, was reintroduced into the cities from the villages.

Thousands and then millions of people began to spin their own Indian cloth from Indian wool and cotton, or they bought their clothing from Indians who did. The spinning wheel, like the defiance of the Salt Law, became a symbol of national honor, dignity, and solidarity.

Within thirty days following Gandhi's disobedience of the Salt Law at Dandi, the entire country seemed to be acting as a single person in its defiance of the government. Except for freakish and isolated acts of violence on the part of a few Indians, the entire campaign was carried out nonviolently and in the true spirit of satyagraha.

Finally on the night of May 4th, armed Indian policemen led by a British magistrate came to Gandhi's camp near Dandi and arrested him. Gandhi was given permission to brush his teeth while the arrest order was read. He said his prayers, the satyagrahis around the encampment sang a hymn, and Mohandas Karamchand Gandhi was taken off to a waiting truck and from there to prison.

Some Accomplishments

Though the Salt Law was not repealed until one year later, the satyagraha salt campaign of 1930 accomplished three things. First, it demonstrated that satyagraha could be used on a massive scale to draw worldwide attention to Indian social injustices and political persecution. The conscience of the world community could be aroused by such a simple, elemental act as making salt when the laws prohibiting it were embedded in a wider and more massive net of social and political injustice.

Second, it demonstrated that satyagraha as a nonviolent instrument of action could unite a people more securely, more unselfishly, than could a massive violent campaign. In meeting force, violence, and hatred with love, nonviolence, and passive resistance, the Indians blunted the edges of the violent weapons used by their oppressors. Public and individual responses to the new instrument of liberation defeated the British more effectively than bombs and bullets ever could have.

Third, and finally, it demonstrated that Indians, held together by a common love rather than a common hatred, could, if they could defeat the British, face any power on earth. They were demonstrating that love, trust, selflessness, and nonviolence could move the hearts of men and, as a consequence, move whole nations and the entire world. They suddenly found that this bond of love united them more surely as a nation than any religion, creed, or philosophy had heretofore been able to do. The Hindu, Christian, Jew, Buddhist, Jain, and Moslem of India discovered a brotherhood beyond their sects and beyond their dogmas, and they realized, perhaps for the first time, what it meant to be an Indian. Satyagraha helped to define them as a people by giving them a common cause and a common means with which to develop that cause. It was the beginning of the modern Republic of India.

The Death of Gandhi

Gandhi believed deeply in his instrument for liberation and used satyagraha numerous times in his struggle for the independence of India. On January 30, 1948, a year after that independence was granted, and while Gandhi was on his way to public prayers, he was shot and killed by an assassin.

With his simple habits of food and dress, with his simple doctrines of love and forgiveness, Gandhi was to become an inspiration to millions of people all over the world (including the late Dr. Martin Luther King, Jr.) who watched admiringly as one man's philosophy moved the mighty British empire. It is out of this tumultuous and strife-ridden worldly activity that Gandhi's prescription for liberation was born.[1]

Self-realization as the Way of Selfless Action

Consider the following: Mohandas Gandhi is asked, Can a man or woman attain self-realization, that is, ultimate happiness or liberation, by mere recitation of *Rāmanāma* (repeating, or meditating on, the name of God, Rāma) and without taking part in worldly actions, such as national service? The questioner (a woman) adds that her sisters have told her that one need not do anything "beyond attending to family requirements and occasionally showing kindness to the poor." The Mahatma (the word "mahātma" is an honorific title meaning "great souled," something like the word "saint") answers:

> This question has puzzled not only women but many men and has taxed me to the utmost. I know that there is a school of philosophy which teaches complete inaction and the futility of all effort. I have

> not been able to appreciate that teaching, unless in order to secure verbal agreement I were to put my own interpretation on it. In my humble opinion *effort* is necessary for one's own growth. It has to be irrespective of results. Ramanama or some equivalent is necessary not for the sake of repetition but for the sake of *purification*, as an aid to effort, for direct *guidance from above*. It is therefore never a substitute for effort. It is meant for intensifying and guiding it in a proper channel. If all effort is vain, why [engage in] family cares or an occasional help to the poor? In this very effort is contained the germ of national service. A national service, to me, means service of humanity, even as *disinterested service* of the family means the same thing. Disinterested service of the family necessarily leads one to national service. Ramanama gives one detachment and ballast and never throws one off one's balance at critical moments. *Self-realization* I hold to be impossible without service of and identification with the poorest.[2]

Mohandas Gandhi's doctrine of satyagraha is captured beautifully in this brief answer quoted from a 1926 editorial column in *Young India,* his own weekly newspaper. That doctrine and that answer are both expressions of a philosophy of action that begins with self-*purification* which, in turn, leads to *disinterested* or unselfish moral *effort* which is, itself, *guided by God*. It is a commitment to a way of doing actions without which self-realization would be impossible. The foundation of this way of action, as we shall see below, is derived primarily from the *Vedas* and the *Bhagavad Gītā*. Before turning to that, however, let us look at our second, and rather different, Indian sage, he whom many have called "the greatest holy man of modern India."

Śri Ramana Bhagavan Maharshi (1879-1950)

Śri (a title that means "honored one") Ramana (Venkataraman was his full name) Maharshi was born some ten years after Gandhi on December 30, 1879, in Tirucculi, South India. The Maharshi's (another honorific name meaning "great sage") brahmin father was an accountant's assistant and later an uncertified legal pleader practicing in magistrate's court. His household, according to tradition, was "cursed" into surrendering one member of the family in each generation to become a monk or sannyāsi (a "renunciate") who would break all attachments to the world and live a life of holy solitude. Ramana was to become that "cursed" member.

His father died when he was twelve and the family moved to Madurai. Ramana attended Scott's Middle School and the American Mission High School until he was sixteen years of age. Like Gandhi and like Bhaktivedanta later, he was not an accomplished student, preferring outdoor sports and games to books and lessons, even though he had a rather remarkable memory and a more than capable mind. It is said that if he heard a classmate recite a lesson, he could subsequently reproduce it perfectly and without mistakes.

Maharshi's Liberation

In 1896, just before he had reached the age of seventeen, an event occurred that was to alter his life dramatically and turn him into one of his generation's, and the world's, greatest religious mystics. Sitting alone one day in his uncle's house, he suddenly had the horrible but unmistakable feeling that he was about to die. He lay down and stretched out, holding his body stiff and straight. Stopping his breath and closing his eyes, he became, as he afterward recounted, "a corpse." But then he thought:

> Well, this body is now dead. It will be carried to the funeral pyre and there reduced to ashes. But do I die with the death of this body? Is the body I? It is silent and inert; but I feel the full force of my personality and even the voice of the "I" within me, apart from it. So I am the Spirit transcending the body. The body dies but the Spirit that transcends it cannot be touched by death. That means that I am the deathless Spirit.[3]

Suddenly, the knowledge of Who he was came to him in an instantaneous flash. The fear of death vanished entirely. He had reached that goal called *mokṣa* ("release" or "liberation") that so many Hindus believe that it takes lifetimes to find. It was August 29, 1896.

The moksa experience produced a complete change in the young saint's life. T.M.P. Mahadevan described that life.

> The things that he had valued before now lost their meaning. The spiritual values which he had ignored till then became the only objects of attention. School studies, friends, relations no longer had any significance for him. He became utterly indifferent to his surroundings. Humility, meekness, passivity and other virtues came to be his characteristics. Avoiding company he preferred to sit alone, absorbed in concentration on the Self. He went to the Minaksi temple every day, and was exalted whenever he stood before the images of the gods and the saints. Tears flowed from his eyes profusely. The new vision was constantly with him. His was the transfigured life.[4]

One day, six weeks after this transforming event, he sat in school, bored and disinterested. As punishment for his lack of attention, his English teacher ordered Ramana to copy an exercise three times from Bain's *English Grammar;* the new *Jīvanmukta* ("one who is liberated while still alive") began, and finished the first two copyings before he stopped, struck by the incongruity of it all. Casting aside the copying materials, he sat up, closed his eyes and began his meditation. He realized that his old life was now meaningless and he resolved to leave that life and move on to whatever the world now held for him.

He resolved to go to Tiruvannamalai, a place of pilgrimage that had held some mysterious and mystical attraction for him since he had first heard the name years before. Tiruvannamalai ("Arunācala" in Sanskrit) is 120 miles southwest of Madras and is named after the sacred hill that dominates the town. The hill is sacred to the God Śiva, the Lord of Arunācala. It was at this hill that Śiva had appeared as an endless column of light, represented now by the liṅgam (a "mark" or "sign"), a long, slender phallic-shaped column. The hill itself is said to be the lingam of Śiva, and Arunācala ("the red hill") is the solidified light of God. It is a holy site of pilgrimage for millions of Hindus who come to have *darśan* ("a reverent viewing") and to piously circumambulate the sacred hill as a special act of devotion. Ramana was strangely and compellingly drawn to Arunācala as a boy of seventeen in 1896. After many hardships he finally arrived, and there he remained, attracting loving attention, admirers, and devotees from around the world until his death from cancer in 1950.[5]

The famous and the obscure journeyed to Arunācala to catch a glimpse of the God-realized saint. F. H. Humphreys was the first

European to meet the new Maharshi in an encounter that took place in November of 1911. Humphreys recorded his first impressions:

> At two o'clock in the afternoon we went up the hill to see him. On reaching the cave [Maharshi resided in a cave the first seventeen years at Arunacala] we sat before him, at his feet, and said nothing. We sat thus for a long time and I felt lifted out of myself. For half an hour I looked into the Maharshi's eyes, which never changed their expression of deep contemplation. I began to realize somewhat that the body is the temple of the Holy Ghost; I could only feel that his body was not the man; it was the instrument of God, merely a sitting motionless corpse from which God was radiating terrifically. My own feelings were indescribable.[6]

Humphreys was subsequently followed by hundreds of other Europeans including Paul Brunton in 1931 and W. Somerset Maugham in 1936.

One Indian visitor, T.M.P. Mahadevan, records his feelings at first visiting Maharshi when Mahadevan himself was only eighteen:

> It was a delightful and unique experience to sit in the presence of the Maharshi, and look at the full glare of the radiant eyes. One might go to him with a medley of doubts and questions, but very often it happened that these upsurgings of the mind died down and were burnt to ashes as one sat before the sage. One had a foretaste of that pristine state, of which the *Upaniṣad* speaks, when the knot of the heart is cut and all doubts are dispelled. One stepped back and watched how the turbulent mental stream quietened down, and received the undisturbed reflection of the self-luminous Spirit.[7]

More pilgrims began to make the journey to Arunācala to have darśan of Maharshi. And they came with questions, problems, and concerns that they felt only the great Jīvanmukta himself could answer. T.M.P. Mahadevan catalogues the requests:

> Some went to the Maharshi curious to get from him a cure-all for the world's ills. The used to ask him what solution he had for the problems of poverty, illiteracy, disease, war, etc. Social reform was their religion; a reordering of society was what they sought. They framed their questions in different ways. What message had the

> Maharshi to give to the social reformer? Was it not the duty of every enlightened citizen to strive for bettering the lot of his fellowmen? When misery and squalor were abroad, how could anyone who had a feeling heart keep quiet without exerting himself by doing his bit for world welfare?[8]

And how did Maharshi respond to these social concerns by these would-be social reformers?

> An invariable answer that the sage gave to all those who put such questions was: "Have you reformed yourself first?"[9]

For was it not the case, he asked, that much social action is merely a form of ego gratification? Was it not the case that so-called altruism and concern for one's neighbor are simply excuses to build power for oneself and exercise the ego? For it is the ego with its desires and its ignorance that stands as the chief obstacle, as we shall see, to Self-realization or mokṣa:

> And so, unless one seeks to know the true Self, one cannot really serve society. Reform must begin with oneself.[10]

The issue is important and we shall see Maharshi in action, shortly, as he answers a disciple's question about Self-realization (as opposed to Gandhi's *self*-realization) and social reform.

Maharshi was subsequently feted by the German Indologist, Heinrich Zimmer, and the Swiss psychologist and polymath, Carl G. Jung. The latter had praised Maharshi as the perfect "embodiment of spiritual India" and as "the whitest spot on a white surface." In Maharshi there is "purest India, the breath of eternity, scorning and scorned by the world." Jung continues:

> It is the song of the ages, resounding, like the shrilling crickets on a summer's night, from a million beings. This melody is built upon one great theme, which veiling its monotony under a thousand colorful reflections, tirelessly and everlastingly rejuvenates itself in the Indian spirit, whose youngest incarnation is Śri Ramana himself.[11]

Whatever system of thought Maharshi accepted rests upon the realization of the Self. And the way to that Self lies in meditation on the question, Who am I? The matter has been put most succinctly by Robert A. McDermott and V. S. Naravane:

> The key to Śri Ramana's guidance is the silence which can be achieved by inquiring into the thought, "Who am I?" In this way, the I can be seized, controlled, and shown to be a manifestation of Self; ultimately it can be shown that "I," along with the world, God, and other parts of reality are all the Self. Silence allows this identity to be established.[12]

This expression of Maharshi's philosophy regarding the Self, its realization, and the silence (or meditation) necessary to that end is, as we shall see, Upaniṣadic in origin. But Maharshi does not so much confirm that Upaniṣadic teaching by his experiences as the *Upaniṣads* themselves confirm Maharshi's experiences. It is a question of priorities, really, for, in this case, Maharshi's experience of the Self came before his study of the *Upaniṣads*.

Self-realization as the Way of Mystical Knowledge

Now consider the following: The Sage of Arunācala, as Ramana Maharshi came to be called, is asked a question about Self-realization or mokṣa. The question occurs in a dialogue between a disciple, 'D', and Maharshi, 'M':

> D. How can I attain Self-realization?
>
> M. Realization is nothing to be gained afresh; it is already there. All that is necessary is to get rid of the thought 'I have not realized.' Stillness or Peace is Realization. There is no moment when the Self is not. So long as there is doubt or the feeling of non-Realization, the attempt should be made to rid oneself of these thoughts. They are due to the identification of the Self with the not-Self. When the not-Self disappears, the Self alone remains. To make room it is enough that the cramping be removed; room is not brought in from elsewhere.
>
> D. Since Realization is not possible without *vasana-kshaya* [the destruction (kṣaya) of unconscious and latent desires (vāsanās)]

how am I to realize that State in which the vasanas are effectively destroyed?

M. You are in that State now!

D. Does it mean that by holding on to the Self, the vasanas should be destroyed as and when they emerge?

M. They will themselves be destroyed if you remain as you are.

D. How shall I reach the Self?

M. There is no reaching the Self. If Self were to be reached, it would mean that the Self is not here and now but that it is yet to be obtained....

The Self, or *Ātman,* is the Holy Power, or Brahman, of the universe, impersonal and real but indescribable. To know or realize It or That, as opposed to He or She, is to be liberated forever. But does such liberation help the world?

D. Does my Realization help others? [the earnest disciple asks]

M. Yes, and it is the best help that you can possibly render to others. Those who have discovered great truths have done so in the still depths of the Self. *But really there are no 'others' to be helped.* For the Realized Being sees only the Self, just as the goldsmith sees only the gold while valuing it in various jewels made of gold. When you identify yourself with the body, name and form are there. But when you transcend the body-consciousness, the 'others' also disappear. *The Realized One does not see the world as different from Himself.*

D. Would it not be better if the Saints mix with others?

M. *There are no 'others' to mix with.* The Self is the only Reality.

D. Should I not try to help the suffering world?

M. The Power that created you has created the world as well. If it can take care of you, It can similarly take care of the world also.... *If God has created the world, it is His business to look after it, not yours.*

D. Is it not our duty to be patriots?

M. Your duty is TO BE and not to be this or that. "I AM THAT I AM" sums up the whole truth: the method is summarized in 'BE STILL.' And what does Stillness mean? It means 'Destroy yourself'; because, every name and form is the cause of trouble. 'I-I' is the Self. 'I am this' is the ego. When the 'I' is kept up as the 'I' only, it is the Self. When it flies off at a tangent and says 'I am this or that, I am such and such,' -- it is the ego.

D. Who then is God?

M. The Self is God. 'I AM' is God. If God be apart from the Self, He must be a Selfless God, which is absurd.
ALL that is required to realize the Self is to BE STILL. What can be easier than that? Hence *Atma-vidya* [knowledge of the real Self] is the easiest to attain.[13]

In a sense Maharshi's entire philosophy is, as the quote from Gandhi was previously, compressed into this brief excerpt. And it will be our task to seek the roots of this philosophy, a philosophy that has been aptly named *advaita* (nondualistic) *Vedānta*, in the foundations of Hinduism.

Advaita is a doctrine of stillness that seeks the pure state of real Being or God in the quiet and depths of the Self, and it is that search that leads ultimately to Self-realization or mokṣa. The foundation of this philosophy of stillness, as we shall see below, is found primarily in the *Upaniṣads.*

Gandhi and Maharshi Compared

Gandhi and Maharshi would seem to differ profoundly on the place of action and stillness in solving human problems. Although Gandhi, as we have seen, placed self-realization, his ultimate solution to the problem of suffering, in social action, Maharshi found his Self-realization through being still and letting God look after the suffering world. The ways of action and stillness in solving human problems reflect attitudes and doctrines certainly familiar even to Western men and women. Gandhi's way of action (works) and Maharshi's way of stillness (knowledge) are mirrored in the social and monastic traditions of both Christianity and Western society.

The way of action encompasses a social gospel that says essentially that all of us have a holy mission to prevent or reduce human suffering in the world, a view made popular (and unpopular) by radical reformers and revolutionaries from St. Francis of Assisi to Martin Luther King, Jr., of Birmingham to Dorothy Day of New York and Mother Teresa of Calcutta. Here is the Reverend Martin Luther King,

Jr., a man profoundly influenced by the life and writings of Mohandas Gandhi, speaking as a Christian satyagrahi:

> Any religion that professes to be concerned about the souls of men and is not concerned about the slums that damn them, the economic conditions that strangle them and the social conditions that cripple them is a spiritually moribund religion awaiting burial.[14]

The way of stillness and mystical knowledge, on the other hand, encompasses the monastic gospel that says essentially that the world is the place of Satan or a mere bridge upon which one must not build, a view made popular by mystics and contemplatives from St. Benedict to Meister Johannes Eckhart to William Law and Thomas Merton.

The mystical contemplative way of knowledge has been all but lost in the West as the way of action has become even more stridently popular. It is apparently easier to understand a Gandhi or a King than it is to understand a Maharshi or a Merton. Here is the late Father Thomas Merton, a man profoundly influenced by the Western mystical tradition and Zen Buddhism, speaking about the great German theologian and jñāna yogi, Meister Eckhart (1260-1327):

> A fuller and truer expression of Zen [mysticism] in Christian experience is given by Meister Eckhart. He admits that: "To be a proper abode for God and fit for God to act in, a man should also be free from all things and actions, both inwardly and outwardly." But now Eckhart goes on to say that there is much more: "A man should be so poor ["*voluntary* poverty" is Eckhart's sermon topic] that he is not and has not a place for God to act in. To reserve a place would be to maintain distinctions."[15]

In other words, God and man have become One, there are no "others."

But there is a third way, the way of devotion to God, that teaches that there is a fundamental incompleteness and wrongheadedness about both the way of selfless action and the way of mystical knowledge, in solving human problems. This way is best represented in the life and writings of a man who might easily be called the most well-known missionary of devotional Hinduism in the 20th century--Swami A. C. Bhaktivedanta.

A. C. Bhaktivedanta Swami Prabhupáda (1896-1977)

Swami ("master") A. C. Bhaktivedanta was born Abhay Charan De in a Calcutta suburb in 1896. Abhay's father was a cloth merchant belonging by birth to the suvarna-vanik merchant class or *varṇa*. More importantly, the father was also a devout *Vaiṣṇava,* a worshipper of the Hindu God Viṣṇu and His human incarnation, Lord Kṛṣṇa. As a Vaiṣṇava, the father never touched meat, eggs, fish, coffee, or tea, a practice his son was to follow. The father's religious devotion and ideas were easily impressed upon the young son and Abhay grew up surrounded by all the trappings of the bhakti, or devotional, tradition of strict but loving service to Lord Kṛṣṇa. This life in service to God included daily prayers and rituals together with the recitations from the *Caitanya-caritāmṛta,* the life of Lord Chaitanya Mahāprabhu, a Bengali saint of the sixteenth century, and from the devotional literature written by and about other great Bengali Vaiṣṇavas of the past. These latter included recitations from the *Śrīmad-Bhāgavatam* (the stories and recountings of Lord Kṛṣṇa's life on earth composed by Śrīla Vyāsadeva), along with chants with japa beads, as well as offerings of *pūjā* or ceremonial worship in front of the image of Lord Kṛṣṇa. It was a devoutly religious family, indeed, in which the young Abhay was raised.

By his own accounts, Abhay was a naughty, spoiled, and pampered child. But he was, at the same time, the most loved of the four children in Papa De's family. An incident in his childhood is amusing but not untypical:

> One day in the market he saw a toy gun he wanted. His father said no, and Abhay started to cry. "All right, all right," Gour Mohan said, and he bought the gun. Then Abhay wanted another gun.... "One for each hand," Abhay cried, and he lay down in the street, kicking his feet. When Gour Mohan agreed to get the second gun, Abhay was pacified.[16]

In 1916 Abhay began college and in 1918 he married Radharani Datta, a girl of eleven, the daughter of a prominent gold merchant. He was later to admit, following a not altogether happy marriage that included several children, that he had never really liked Radharani. He completed his college work by 1920 but did not accept his B. A.

diploma, opting instead to join in the popular protest against British occupation and colonial policies in his country. In 1921 he began work in Calcutta as a department manager in the pharmaceutical firm of Dr. Patrick Chandra Bose. He was to remain attached to Bose and pharmaceuticals, first as a respected employee and later as the owner of a very prosperous drug company, for the next 35 years.

Abhay De's Conversion

In 1922 an event occurred that was subsequently to change the direction of his entire life. Abhay met, and in his heart accepted as his own spiritual guru, one of the great Vaiṣṇava sannyāsis of modern India, Śrīla Bhaktisiddhānta Sarasvatī. This man had renounced the world in favor of the spiritual life of a wandering missionary utterly dedicated to the service of Lord Kṛṣṇa. Śrīla Bhaktisiddhānta was especially controversial for he believed that the varṇa or vocational caste that one belongs to is a matter, not of birth, but of the state of one's heart, a condition of inwardness. We shall explore the scriptural grounds for this claim shortly. Śrīla Bhaktisiddhānta believed, furthermore, that he was able to determine who had achieved this state of inwardness. In an elaborate ceremony he initiated nonbrahmins, that is, persons who were not by birth called to be priests and teachers of the sacred Hindu *Vedas,* turning them into bona fide brahmins. As brahmins, these non-bramins-by-birth could, as brahmins-by-initiation, now conduct Hindu religious rites and ceremonies and initiate other non-brahmins-by-birth to the ranks of brahmins-by-initiation. Many Hindus were deeply disturbed by the practice and Śrīla Bhaktisiddhānta was persecuted for his beliefs.

In 1932 Abhay himself received the brahmin initiation from Śrīla Bhaktisiddhānta but remained with his pharmaceutical business, moving to Bombay in 1933. In late 1936 Śrīla Bhaktisiddhānta ordered his lay pupil to preach the message of Lord Chaitanya in English. A year later the master died and Abhay began to be both haunted and inspired by his master's last request to him. In 1939 his brothers in the movement begun by Bhaktisiddhānta conferred upon Abhay the title of "Bhaktivedanta." It was to mark another turning point for his life. Bhaktivedanta discovered he had a gift for writing and over the next twenty years, in addition to giving moral, physical, and financial support to the movement, he was to write, publish, and edit numerous pamphlets, journals, and books all aimed at extending the teaching of Lord Kṛṣṇa. Gradually, family duties and business responsibilities became especially burdensome. In 1954 he left his family and his business in order to devote all of his energies to doing what his master had charged him to do, preach the message of Lord Chaitanya in English.

On September 17, 1959, in imitation of his own master, he was formally initiated into the sannyāsa order, the order of wandering preachers who have given up all attachment to the world. It was to be the prelude to his momentous journey to the West. Thus it was that in 1965, feeling that it had been his master's wish that he bring the message of Lord Chaitanya and Lord Kṛṣṇa to the English-speaking world, Swami Bhaktivedanta set sail from Calcutta for the United States.

All alone but firmly believing that God- or Kṛṣṇa-consciousness was the only answer to the evils of the modern, unhappy, atheistic, materialistic, and pain-wracked world, Swami Bhaktivedanta landed in New York City intent on preaching that God-consciousness to whoever would listen. He was nearly seventy years of age.

Bhaktivedanta opened a storefront mission in the Bowery and began to work with and preach Kṛṣṇa-consciousness to the bums, hippies, drug users, and straights that came to his refuge out of either desperation or curiosity. He began to train an order of monks and nuns that, like himself, ate no meat, fish, or eggs, that rejected intoxicants of all sorts from tea to heroin, and that renounced illicit sex, gambling, and stealing, along with other minor and major vices. Focusing his thoughts, ministry, and beliefs on the myths, stories, and views of Kṛṣṇa and Chaitanya Mahāprabhu, and now ordering his own disciples to do the same, the movement known as Kṛṣṇa Consciousness began to grow and develop. Just as gradually, his own interpretation of the religion and philosophy of Lord Kṛṣṇa and of Śrīla Chaitanya began to take form as well. Perhaps a word about both Kṛṣṇa and Chaitanya would be in order at this point.

Kṛṣṇa-realization as the Way of Devotion

Lord Kṛṣṇa's Life and Death.

The particular tradition to which Bhaktivedanta had been attached since childhood probably had its origins in the early Buddhist period, 400-200 B.C.E. In the beginning, Kṛṣṇa was probably a non-Āryan folk hero, and hence he and the legends about him were very likely non-Vedic and nonbrahmin in origin.[17]

About the first century C.E. more legends were added to the earlier story of Kṛṣṇa's birth and life. These legends depict the beautiful child Kṛṣṇa as the favorite of the cowherds and milkmaids of Brindaban (or Vṛndāvana), a grove in the Mathura district near Kṛṣṇa's village, attempts by demons and ogres to kill him, and his moral battles with the God Indra. By the sixth century the legends were expanded to include his loving exploits with the milkmaids (gopīs) of Brindaban. By the ninth and tenth centuries these exploits had evolved into the erotic adventures of Kṛṣṇa as described in the tenth century C.E. *Bhāgavata Purāṇa,* a work of devotional literature that described the dual routes of bhakti through maternal and sexual love.

The story was that King Kaṃsa, the tyrant cousin of the Princess Devakī, heard a prophecy that Devakī's eighth child was fated to kill him. Kaṃsa is only prevented from killing Devakī right then and there on the promise from her husband that he would give every infant born of his wife to Kaṃsa. Kaṃsa agrees. After killing six of the infants from Devakī's womb, he is initially tricked into believing that the seventh is a miscarriage when actually it is Kṛṣṇa's brother who is born and who survives. Subsequently, following another elaborate subterfuge, Kṛṣṇa, the eighth child, is born and exchanged for another child before Kaṃsa can discover his error. Lord Kṛṣṇa's birth from Princess Devakī is recorded in the *Harivaṁśa,* a text of the fifth century C.E.:

> At that moment, in the very middle of the night, when the moon was in 'Victorious,' the oceans shook and the mountains trembled, and the fires blazed peacefully, when the Exciter of Men was born. Gentle winds blew, and the dust lay undisturbed, and the stars shone brightly, when the Exciter was born. Drums which had not been struck resounded to the heaven of the gods, and the lord of the triple heaven sent down a rain of flowers from the sky.[18]

The infant Kṛṣṇa is raised by a cowherdsman, Nanda, and his wife, Yaśodā, for it was their own child that had been exchanged for the infant Kṛṣṇa and then murdered. But Kṛṣṇa's troubles are by no means over. Kaṃsa learns of the child's existence and sends a horrible ogress, Pūtanā, to kill him. Pūtanā travels the countryside killing infants. Half mammal, half bird, she flies through the air seeking victims whose parents have not recited the deeds of Kṛṣṇa. Disguised as a beautiful woman, Pūtanā enters Nanda's house and, seeing the infant Kṛṣṇa, seeks to devour him. Yaśodā is completely taken in by the beauty of the visitor but the infant, even with his eyes closed, immediately recognizes Pūtanā. Taking Kṛṣṇa on her lap she offers her breast to the infant to suck having just smeared it with a deadly poison. But, seizing the breast, the youthful God sucks the life out of his attacker, instead. The surrounding mountains and hills shake and then the entire earth itself and the sky and planets quake, echoing and resounding with her horrific screams as she dies. And there is the infant Kṛṣṇa sitting on her fallen corpse, playing, wholly without fear. His mother snatches him up and the other wives of the cowherds marvel at the event they have just witnessed. Quickly the motherly protectors of the courageous young Lord bathe him, feed him, and put him to bed.

Pūtanā's body is cut up and burned but her soul goes to heaven for she had given her breast to Kṛṣṇa, even though it was to kill him. And the *Bhāgavata Purāṇa,* the devotional text from which the story of Kṛṣṇa and Pūtanā comes, is quick to draw the moral:

> How much greater, then, is the reward of those who offer what is dearest to the highest Soul, Kṛṣṇa, with faith and devotion, like his doting mothers? She [Pūtanā] gave her breast to Kṛṣṇa to suck, and he touched her body with his two feet which remain in the hearts of his devotees and which are adored by those who are adored by the world, and so, though an evil sorceress, she obtained the heaven which is the reward of mothers. What then is the reward of those cows and mothers whose breasts' milk Kṛṣṇa drank?... Since they always looked upon Kṛṣṇa as their son, they will never again be doomed to rebirth that arises from ignorance.[19]

This story concludes with the auspicious reminder:

> Whatever mortal faithfully hears this tale of the marvelous deed of the baby Kṛṣṇa, the liberation of Pūtanā, he finds his joy in Govinda [the good "Cowherd," like the good Shepherd from another tradition].[20]

Kṛṣṇa's life is given in some detail throughout the bhakti texts of the *Purāṇas* of the years 400-900 C.E. There is the story of the gopī's (here symbolizing the devotees of Kṛṣṇa) and their stolen clothes, their nakedness symbolizing the emptiness of self with which the adoring worshippers must approach their beloved Lord. One day the gopīs had gone to the river. The young maidens are all sick with love for the handsome young man of the village and each desires to marry him. Removing their clothing, they step into the river to play and to bathe. Kṛṣṇa appears and laughingly steals all of their clothes. Climbing a tree, he shouts to the girls, who cover their bareness with the river. He invites each one to come to him and get their clothes. Filled with love but shy from their nakedness, they tell him that he has played a wicked trick on them. They tell him that they are his slaves and will obey him but that nudity and decency forbid. 'Then come and get your clothes if you are my slaves,' he taunts them. He compels them to bow down to him after placing their hands on their heads, thereby exposing their full nakedness to him: Devotees must reveal all to their lord, concealing nothing. The gopīs comply and he gives them their clothes. The point of the *Bhāgavata Purāṇa* story is, of course, a point about bhakti:

> Though they were greatly deceived and robbed of their modesty, though they were mocked and treated like toys and stripped of their clothes, yet they held no grudge against him, for they were happy to be together with their beloved. Rejoicing in the closeness of their lover, they put on their clothes....

Then the young God speaks to them:

> Good ladies, I know that your desire is to worship me. I rejoice in this vow, which deserves to be fulfilled. The desire of those whose hearts have been placed in me does not give rise to further desire,...[21]

Kṛṣṇa grows to manhood and with his brother returns to Mathura where, after many adventures fighting beasts, ogres, and demons, he slays the wicked Kaṃsa, as had been foretold. After placing a just man on the throne, he then journeys to Dvārakā and sets up his own kingdom. Kṛṣṇa then heroically participates in the great fratricidal battle between the Pāṇḍavas and the Kauravas, the story that is partially described in the *Bhagavad Gītā.* By strategies, prowess, and deceptions Kṛṣṇa helps the Pāṇḍavas to victory as the charioteer of the Pāṇḍava hero, Arjuna. Kṛṣṇa's life ends in a tragic way when, mistaken for a deer, a hunter shoots him in his foot, the one vulnerable part of his body.

This, then, is the mythic foundation on which the later worship and adoration of Kṛṣṇa as Lord Kṛṣṇa will be built. One of the most important worshippers in that tradition was a Bengali brahmin by the name of Chaitanya (*Caitanya* in Sanskrit). His life and way of liberation from suffering will have a profound effect on Hindu devotionalism, in general, and on Bhaktivedanta, in particular.

Chaitanya and Bengali Bhaktism

Bhakti flowered in the sixteenth century in Bengal and subsequently throughout India due largely to the efforts of one man. Born in 1485, Chaitanya was a twenty-two-year-old brahmin scholar from Navadvipa when he was converted to Vaiṣṇavism while on a trip to perform funeral rites for his dead father at Gaya. He returned home to Navadvipa totally changed by his experience, gave up the scholarly brahminical life that he had been living in order to devote himself totally to the praise of Kṛṣṇa and to the chanting of Kṛṣṇa's holy name. He organized *saṅkīrtanas* (community chantings in honor of Lord Kṛṣṇa) and after two years became a sannyāsi. He spent the next six years traveling and converting all whom he met to Vaiṣṇavism. The remaining eighteen years of his life were lived in Puri preaching the holy love of Kṛṣṇa and entering into ecstatic trances suffering the tortures of separation from his beloved Lord.

His singing became an emotional, near-hysterical outpouring of his love for the God whom he worshipped. He shouted, wept, danced, and sang, attracting followers first by his curiously uncontrolled enthusiasm and then by his sincere and utter devotion to God. His ecstatic yearning to be joined with his beloved Kṛṣṇa often ended in epileptic seizures in which his arms became rigid as he fell to the ground, his mouth foamed, his eyes rolled back in his head, and his mind was swept into unconscious and joyful union with his God. Chaitanya's life was sadly ended, according to one account, when he drowned in a frenzied epileptic attack while bathing in the ocean near Puri.

Chaitanya laid the foundation of modern Vaiṣṇavism with doctrines that were later incorporated into the Kṛṣṇa Consciousness movement by Bhaktivedanta and his own teachers. Chaitanya introduced a strange type of self-intoxicating song-dance called *kīrtana*; he imitated the episodes in the life of Kṛṣṇa as recited in the *Purāṇas;* he denounced the metaphysical monism of the *Upaniṣads,* wherein the self is absorbed into impersonal Brahman, as wrongheaded; he rejected the *Vedas,* in general, as antithetical to the grace and love of God. In other words, neither the way of sacrifice and action, Gandhi's way, nor the way of knowledge and absorption, Maharshi's way, would have appealed to Chaitanya. He revived the hypnotic emotionalism of the love between Kṛṣṇa and his female/feminine consort or counterpart, Rādhā. The highest kind of love became that wherein both lover and beloved melt into one, losing their individuality in the 'sweet milky flow of love.'

After Chaitanya's death, Brindaban, the place of Kṛṣṇa's early life, was rebuilt and a temple erected there by Chaitanya's followers. Though he had repudiated all caste distinctions, allowing any and all persons to become bhaktas of Lord Kṛṣṇa, these same followers now established a regular hereditary priesthood called *Goswamis,* "cow masters," with all the prejudices and distinctions then present in the more orthodox Hindu tradition. Chaitanya himself became an object of adoration and then, as a reincarnation of Lord Kṛṣṇa, he began to be worshipped as Lord Kṛṣṇa.

Chaitanya appears to have held the following four significant views. First, Brahman is a Person and He possesses all possible power, *śakti,* within Himself: He has the powers of bliss or ultimate enjoyment, being, and consciousness within Himself; He is the power and controller within the selves of all individuals, i.e., He lives within all beings; He is the power by which the phenomenal world is created. In other words, Brahman is personal and transcendent; He is the immanent God within each person; and He is the Creator of the phenomenal universe.

Second, the highest state of devotional service that man can reach is through his renouncing of all other interests through utter devotion to God alone. In other words, the best possible condition for man is one in which he renounces all duties, whether toward caste or community or family, and accepts only those duties to God alone.

Third, the absolute devotion to God is exclusive of both knowledge of God and sacrificial action. At this point, Chaitanya appeared to reject, as we have seen, both the way of knowledge as well as the way of action in favor of total and absolute bhakti to Kṛṣṇa.

Of knowledge Chaitanya's attitude is nicely summarized by Surendranath Dasgupta:

> Pure devotion should not have, however, any of the obstructive influences of knowledge; philosophical knowledge and mere disinclination [renunciation] obstruct the course of bhakti.[22]

But once bhakti has revealed the Beloved, then knowledge of His nature may also be fully revealed and actions in His service may be undertaken.

Of action Chaitanya's attitude is, once again, well put by Dasgupta:

> Later on, in *Madhya-līlā*, chapter xxix, Caitanya, in describing the nature of suddha bhakti (pure devotion), says that pure devotion is that in which the devotee renounces all desires, all formal worship, all knowledge and work, and is attached to Kṛṣṇa with all his sense-faculties. A true devotee does not want anything from God, but is satisfied only in loving Him.[23]

Again, service or action, like knowledge or wisdom, may come but only after the bhaktic rendezvous with or in God. In other words, neither knowledge nor action can accomplish for the devotee what pure unobstructed devotion can; moreover, both knowledge and action can retard, if not destroy, the attainment of that ultimate bhaktic goal--union with the Beloved.

Fourth, the devotee to Kṛṣṇa must possess certain preliminary moral qualities in order that the intensity of love to Kṛṣṇa will not be distracted by nor diminished by immoral actions, and in order that that love may continue to grow. Consequently, the devotee must be kind, humble, truthful, noninjurious, magnanimous, tender, pure, selfless, treating all equally while at peace with himself and others. The devotee must associate only with other devotees, clinging to Kṛṣṇa alone as his only support, controlling his passions, making no effort other than to worship Kṛṣṇa.

Swami Bhaktivedanta will follow Śrīla Chaitanya completely in espousing all four of these religious views.

Later Life and ISKCON

In a Bowery loft, with two heart attacks behind him, the seventy-year-old Swami held his own first American kīrtana, a congregational chanting of the name "Hare (pronounced "haray") Kṛṣṇa" (Lord Kṛṣṇa). The news media quickly caught him up and his charitable work with drug users and hippies became widely known. The authoritative chant that his followers continue to use even to this day in the dozens of centers around the world established by ISKCON, the International Society for Krishna Consciousness, and in airports, bus terminals, and other public and private assemblies, is known as the *mahā-mantra:*

> Hare Kṛṣṇa, Hare Kṛṣṇa,
> Kṛṣṇa Kṛṣṇa, Hare Hare.
>
> Hare Rāma, Hare Rāma,
> Rāma Rāma, Hare Hare.

The mahā-mantra is repeated for a traditional 64 rounds, producing a rather delightful sound, lulling the mind with its steady rhythm and leading to, if the mantra is done correctly, ecstatic states of consciousness.

Early in 1967 the Swami flew from New York to San Francisco to begin a second center for Kṛṣṇa Consciousness. In the notorious drop-out drug-in district of Haight-Ashbury, where tens of thousands of hippies had gathered for a "summer of love," Bhaktivedanta began to set up shop to bring chanting, consciousness, bliss, and salvation to America's new lost generation. Again, by all accounts, he was enormously popular as he became associated with rock groups and the sights, sounds, and symbols that were loved by the young people:

> When confronting couples who lived as boyfriend and girlfriend, Śrīla Prabhupāda [as he was now known] asked them to become his married disciples. He agreed to go to a psychedelic dance hall and chant Hare Kṛṣṇa with the Grateful Dead, the Jefferson Airplane, and other rock groups.[24]

Overcoming yet another heart attack in May 1967, Bhaktivedanta returned briefly to India, following which he began an around the world tour. He came back to the United States in December as the sole leader of fifty disciples and six ISKCON centers.[25] The next years were spent traveling the United States and India, speaking on radio, television, and to news reporters, making records, meeting and discipling the Beatles' George Harrison and John Lennon, writing books, going out to the people in preparation for the time when the temples and centers would be constructed and the people would come to him.

The end came in Brindaban, the place sacred to both Lord Kṛṣṇa and Śrīla Chaitanya, on November 14, 1977. In the evening Bhaktivedanta spoke from his bed to the gathered disciples on the subject of how to die through total dependency on Lord Kṛṣṇa. A bit later he was asked by one of the gathered company, "Is there anything you want?" Knowing that anyone who dies in Brindaban is liberated, the good Swami answered, and these were his final words, "I have no desire."

Today the neo-Hindu missionary organization that Bhaktivedanta founded, the International Society of Krishna Consciousness, would appear to accept the following four principles which, paralleling a similar movement within Christianity, we might denominate "Fundamentalist Krishnaism."

First, Lord Kṛṣṇa is the *only* supreme yet personal Lord of the universe. There is no other supreme Lord. Here ISKCON differs from other Vaiṣṇavite sects which hold Viṣṇu as supreme Lord and Kṛṣṇa as merely one of the many incarnations of Him, for example, Buddha and Jesus Christ.[26]

Second, the *Vedas, Upaniṣads,* and the *Bhagavad Gītā* are all *literally* true. The official recounting of the lives of Lord Kṛṣṇa is also to be taken as historically accurate as is the succession of saints and teachers who bear the literal truth in an historical line traceable from

Bhaktivedanta back to Lord Kṛṣṇa himself. These teachers and saints alone carry the truth and they alone teach the truth about the scriptures and about Kṛṣṇa.

Third, only devotional ecstasy directed to Lord Kṛṣṇa leads to liberation and destroys all past wickedness and ignorance. The way of ecstatic bhakti is superior to all other yogas or ways. In addition, all other yogas are false, misleading, and utterly useless in the attainment of liberation.

> Devotionalism is higher to the Krishnaites than yogic or Vedantic meditation [the way of Ramana Maharshi, for example], or moralistic Karma yoga [the way of Gandhi, for example], and definitely better than the much-criticized way of impersonalistic philosophy [the way of secular humanism, for example].[27]

Fourth, the way of devotionalism is difficult but attainable by everyone. Some idea of the difficult demands that the search for devotional ecstasy produces can be seen from the following daily schedule. It is required of those devotees who are considered ministers and wear the saffron robes following a two-and-one-half-year period of training.

3:45 a.m. - rise, shower and dress
4:30 a.m. - chant
5:45 a.m. - read about Kṛṣṇa
8:30 a.m. - communal breakfast
9:00 a.m. - temple cleaning
10:00 a.m. - work; to incense factory, street chanting, etc.
2:00 p.m. - afternoon meal
3:00 p.m. - afternoon work
6:00 p.m. - second shower
7:00 p.m. - evening worship; chanting, dancing, offering
10:00 p.m. - sleep[28]

Much is expected by the devotees but it is obvious that much is expected from them, as well.

How Do You Solve Human Problems?

One question that is bound to occur to the reader regarding these quite different ways or yogas of solving human problems, the way of action and the way of knowledge and the way of devotion, is: Which one is best for solving human problems? Is it by *action,* by *knowledge,* or by *devotion* that problems get solved? And another question immediately arises as well: Which is the best way for Hindus to follow? This question, in turn, leads us back to the question with which this book began and it leads us now into an investigation of the foundations of Hinduism and into the origins of the ways of action, knowledge, and devotion.

We shall call these ways "the devotional way" or "bhaktism" (the religion and philosophy that probably had its origins in pre-Āryan, pre-Vedic India), "the action way" or "brahminism" (the religion and philosophy of the *Vedas*), and "the knowledge way" or "Brahmanism" (the religion and philosophy of the *Upaniṣads*). In addition, these three ways are reflections of the Hindu varṇa or vocational class system and the three quite distinct human attitudes or natures embodied in those classes. Our study will trace the development of the three ways from three historical Indian traditions: first, from the Indus Valley civilization of pre-Āryan India which, we shall argue, may be the source of bhaktism and the devotional way of Hinduism; second, from the *Vedas* which are the source of brahminism and the action way of Hinduism; and third, from the *Upaniṣads* which are the source of Brahmanism and the mystical knowledge way of Hinduism. We will conclude with the *Bhagavad Gītā* which attempts to balance and to blend the three previous ways and, at the same time, to provide a textual foundation for the religion that we know as "Hinduism."

In order to examine these questions about solving human problems and in order to present the ways to solving those problems in as clear and concise a manner as possible, we need a method of analysis and explanation, a sort of heuristic* schema, that will help to give some order and clarity to our investigations into the Hindu ways of solving human problems. The heuristic employed throughout this investigation of Hinduism will be called "the prescription for the liberation from suffering." So before we begin our historical and formal

*A heuristic is something that explains, teaches, or aids and guides discovery; from the Greek *heuriskein,* "to find out."

study of the Hindu ways of solving problems, let us have a look at this heuristic.

The Prescription for the Liberation from Suffering

After his nirvāṇa ("enlightenment") at the age of thirty-five, Gautama the Buddha (563-483 B.C.E.) travelled to Banaras where he delivered his first sermon, the famous "Turning of the Wheel of the Law." In that first sermon, the Buddha compressed all of the essential discoveries that his life and his enlightenment had presented to him into four basic doctrines. These doctrines came to be called "the four noble truths" and they stand at the center of all later Buddhist beliefs, beliefs that might be said to radiate out from these four simple truths.

The Buddha has been likened to a physician diagnosing a disease; and the disease that he found pandemic among all human beings was the disease of *duḥkha* ("suffering"). Here are the four noble truths as enunciated by the Buddha in 528 B.C.:

1. Suffering exists.
2. There is a cause of suffering.
3. Suffering can be stopped.
4. There is a way, the noble eight-fold path, to stop suffering.[29]

I am going to suggest that if all of the essentials of Buddhism can be encompassed in the four noble truths then a similar sort of encompassing can be applied to any religion or any philosophy that sets out to solve human problems. And such a diagnosing as the Buddha performed for Buddhism ought to be applicable to any other religion or philosophy, as we have been using those terms, (see "Preface," p. xiii); recall that we have assumed that both religion and philosophy are disciplines established to solve human problems.

Following the notion that a religion or a philosophy is like a physician's prescription for coping with a disease, let me suggest that we would be able to identify the essentials of any religion or philosophy if we knew, among other things, what the problem was that it was attempting to solve and the way it attempted to solve it. More specifically, let me introduce "the prescription for the liberation from suffering," the name for the heuristic schema that will guide us from diagnosis to cure which, when known, can be used to identify the essentials of any religion or philosophy.

The prescription for the liberation from suffering, or "the Rx* for liberation," in its abbreviated form, assumes two things: first, that "suffering" is the major problem that religions and philosophies have set out to identify and solve; and, second, that "liberation" is the goal at which they are aiming such that when it is reached it would signify that the problem of suffering had been solved. "Suffering" and "liberation" are vague terms and it will be left to our examination of bhaktism in the Indus Valley, to brahminism in the *Vedas,* to Brahmanism in the *Upaniṣads,* and to the synthesis of all three traditions in the *Bhagavad Gītā* to give more precision to these concepts.

Our Rx for liberation will set out to identify the following five things with respect to suffering and its alleviation (consider again those four noble truths of Buddhism and the physician diagnosing a disease):

1. The problem
2. The cause
3. The solution
4. The way to the solution
5. The guiding Principle or Person

Let me speak very briefly of each of these five elements of our Rx for liberation from suffering, and then test the Rx for liberation on Mohandas Gandhi, Ramana Maharshi, and Swami Bhaktivedanta before proceeding with our examination into the historical foundations of Hinduism.

1. The problem. The problem for our religions and philosophies will be "suffering." Suffering may vary from one person to another, and from intense psychological anxiety to acute physical pain, to whatever it is that causes philosophers and sages to lose sleep and their mental equilibrium.

2. The cause. The cause of the problem of suffering for Gandhi, Maharshi, and Bhaktivedanta and for brahminism, Brahmanism, and bhaktism will vary. By

---

*"Rx" is the medical symbol for the Latin word "recipe."

and large there will be three causes of suffering and they will focus on three characteristic failings in the human condition, namely, greed (*lobha*) in brahminism, ignorance (*avidyā* or *ajñāna*) in Brahmanism, and indifference (*pramāda*), which is a function of both greed and ignorance, in bhaktism.

3. The solution. By and large the solution will focus on the ends being sought; for example, heaven for the self in brahminism, mystical absorption for the Self in Brahmanism, and heavenly union with the beloved God in bhaktism.

4. The way. The ways to the solution of the problem of suffering will also vary. By and large the ways will focus on whatever it is that attacks the causes of suffering the best; for example, the control of greed in brahminism, the way of mystical knowledge in Brahmanism, and the desire for God in bhaktism.

5. The guiding Principle or Person. The guiding Principle or Person is that entity that guarantees that if the way to the cause of the problem is followed then the solution will result. By and large the Principle or Person is God, the Gods, or *Ṛta* in brahminism, the law of karma in Brahmanism, and the beloved God or Goddess in bhaktism. Each Principle or Person warrants that if one follows the ways and destroys the causes of the problem then the solution will surely result.

Conclusion

By way of concluding our discussion of the views on self-realization of Mohandas Gandhi, Ramana Maharshi, and A. C. Bhaktivedanta and in order to test our Rx for liberation, suppose that we now apply, quite tentatively, that Rx for liberation to those views.

1. For Gandhi the problem that he sought to solve was the problem of suffering in others. In fact, it is true that Gandhi, Maharshi,

and Bhaktivedanta all sought to end human suffering. But there is a crucial difference. For Gandhi, the "others" that he sought to help were the masses of human beings in South Africa, India, and elsewhere whose suffering was caused by the wretched political, social, and religious practices in which they had become trapped. Thus Gandhi's followers, and Gandhi himself, sought to change or abolish the laws and customs concerning child marriage, untouchability, unjust laws in general, the presence of the British in their country, and so on.

For Maharshi the focus was on his devotees' own suffering; recall that for Maharshi there were in reality no "others" to help. For both Gandhi and Maharshi, however, the goal that they sought remained, ultimately, liberation; but it was their differing conceptions of liberation that set them, and the traditions that they represented within Hinduism, apart from one another.

For Bhaktivedanta the suffering that he sought to end was both his own, as reflected in his separation from God, and the suffering that he found in others, in the people that he encountered and that he regarded as his disciples.

2. For Gandhi the causes of his countrymen's suffering would range from lust, greed, selfishness, poverty, and disease, to child marriage, untouchability, caste discrimination, the presence of a foreign power on Indian soil, and so on. For Maharshi the cause of the problem of one's own suffering lay in ignorance of the Self, one's own true nature. For Bhaktivedanta, the chief causes were indifference to and ignorance of Lord Kṛṣṇa, as well as drugs, crime, and being "turned on" in the wrong way.

3. For Gandhi the solution to the problem of suffering and its causes lay in what I shall call "self-realization" as opposed to Maharshi's solution of "Self-realization" and Bhaktivedanta's "Kṛṣṇa-realization." The difference between self, Self, and Kṛṣṇa will be made clearer as we examine the *Vedas,* where self is emphasized, and the *Upaniṣads,* where Self is emphasized, and the *Gītā,* where Kṛṣṇa is emphasized. For the time being, one can say that for Gandhi liberation, that is, self-liberation, was most often conceived of in terms of bringing heaven to earth; liberation was, therefore, something community-centered, something very practical, very political, and social. Gandhi's philosophy of satyagraha was, after all, action directed; its goals were achieved through direct intervention backed by

prayer and sacrifice, and those goals entailed a change in society, in politics, and in man.

For Maharshi, on the other hand, the solution to the problem of suffering and its cause lay in Self-realization, that is, absorption into Self or Brahman. Maharshi from his cave made it quite clear that for him there was no possibility of putting the search for liberation aside in order to straighten out the world first.

For Bhaktivedanta the solution lay in the devotee's personal experience of his beloved Kṛṣṇa. The ultimate aim was to make that experience eternally continuous.

4. For Gandhi the way to the solution of the problem and the reaching of the goal of heaven, or a better society, or social justice, lay in action and the action prescribed by satyagraha. This action could be directed to man through karma yoga, the yoga of action.

For Maharshi the way to the solution of the problem lay in being still. Where Gandhi's way could be seen as outer-directed, Maharshi's yoga was inner-directed, aiming at the discovery of that pure Being within that he called Self. Being still was achieved through *dhyāna yoga,* the yoga of meditation, on the question, Who am I?, and then through *jñāna yoga,* the yoga of knowledge, one discovered that the Self within was identical with the absolute and transcendent Being of the universe, Brahman.

For Bhaktivedanta the personal experience of Kṛṣṇa was achieved through meditation and the kīrtana in which consciousness of Kṛṣṇa was ecstatically produced.

5. For Gandhi God is the Person Who guarantees that if the ways to the causes of the problem of suffering are followed then the solution will result. In addition, the law of karma, which guarantees that in the long run wickedness gets punished and good efforts never fail, also plays a warranting role for Gandhi, as well as for Maharshi.

For Maharshi Brahman or Self appears to be the Principle that guarantees that if one perseveres in one's silent search for the Self then the solution will result, that is, suffering will end.

For Bhaktivedanta the power of his beloved Lord Kṛṣṇa is able to overcome all obstacles and to guarantee that one's devotional efforts will never be in vain.

In summary, Table 1.1 organizes what we have already said above.

Table 1.1 **The Rx for Liberation from Suffering: Mohandas Gandhi, Ramana Maharshi, and A. C. Bhaktivedanta**

	Mohandas Gandhi (1869-1948)	**Ramana Maharshi** (1879-1950)	**A. C. Bhaktivedanta** (1896-1977)
***Problem*:**	Suffering: The suffering of others	Suffering: One's own suffering	Suffering: One's own and others
***Causes*:**	Greed, selfishness, social injustices, British occupation, etc.	Ignorance of Self	Indifference to Kṛṣṇa; drugs and lust
***Solution*:**	self (as social being)-realization	Self (as Brahman)-realization	Self (as Kṛṣṇa)-realization
***Ways*:**	Satyagraha, karma yoga	Be still, jñāna yoga	Prayer, bhakti yoga
***Guiding Principle or Person*:**	God, the law of karma	Brahman, the law of karma	Lord Kṛṣṇa

We turn next to the foundations of Hinduism in order to pursue the question, now slightly altered, with which this study began: How could these three Hindus--Gandhi, Maharshi, and Bhaktivedanta--hold prescriptions for liberation from suffering that seem so opposed to one another and still be called Hindus? The answer to this question is going to carry us back to the ancient Harappān civilization that existed in India long before the arrival of the people we call "Hindus" and to three of the most sacred compositions of Hinduism. Two of these sacred compositions that we shall be examining are the *Vedas,* in particular the *Ṛg Veda,* and the *Upaniṣads,* in particular the early *Upaniṣads.* These compositions are called *śruti* ("the heard") because they were heard by the *ṛṣis* ("seers") who then transmitted to others what they had "seen"; The *Vedas* and *Upaniṣads* were believed to have been revealed, in other words, rather than created by the ancient seers. Hence, the śruti are said to be eternal and uncreated, existing before even the Gods themselves existed.

The third composition that we shall be examining is the *Bhagavad Gītā.* This work is called *smṛti* ("the remembered") because it was recollected and compiled by one of the great sages of India. This great sage, Vyāsa, might be said to have invented, rather than discovered, the *Gītā.* All three of these compositions are regarded as sacred by the Hindus, however, for through them tradition, Reality, and God speak to all men and women for all time to come.

2

The Foundations of Hinduism: The Harappāns, the *Vedas*, and the *Upaniṣads* (2500-200 B.C.E.)

Sometime between 1800 and 1500 B.C.E. the subcontinent of India was subjected to a series of discrete and limited invasions by a people who called themselves "Āryans" ("noble ones"). These Āryans spoke a language that belongs to what is now called the Indo-European language family, a family that includes such diverse modern European languages as Greek, Latin, German, the Scandinavian languages, French, Spanish, and English. The Āryans came into India from the steppes of Central Asia and from the region to the east of the Caspian Sea. Their invasion occurred at the same time that other members of this same language family were moving out of Central Asia and into ancient Turkey, Greece, and Northern and Southern Europe. The Āryans brought two significant items with them: First, several devastating weapons of war such as the bow and the two-horse chariot, weapons that made them invincible in battle; and, second, their oral compositions that came to be called "the *Vedas.*"

During their very early invasions the Āryans probably encountered the remnants of a once-flourishing and magnificent civilization along the banks of the Indus River, one of the five major rivers of the Punjab and northwestern India. This river culture is called the Harappān or the Indus civilization, and it existed from about 2500 to 1800 B.C.E. Because the Harappān civilization made important bhaktic contributions to Hinduism, let me say a word about it here before we turn our attention to the sacred compositions of their Āryan successors.

The Harappān Civilization (2500-1800 B.C.E.): Bhaktism (The Way of Devotion)

The Cities

The Harappān civilization was a conglomerate of some five large cities and over 150 smaller villages and settlements that flourished from about 2500 to 1800 B.C.E. along the nearly one-thousand-mile stretch of the Indus River and its tributaries. The trading and economic influence of the Indus civilization reached from its source in the northern Punjab to the southern Sind and far out into Sumerian Babylon, Dynastic Egypt, and Minoan Crete. Its religious and cultural influence on later Hinduism has made it one of the four most important river cultures of the ancient world.* The two principal cities of this third millennium culture were Harappā in the Punjab and Mohenjodaro some 400 miles to the south in Sind.

Harappā was first reported by a traveler, Charles Masson, in 1826 ("a ruinous brick castle") but was revealed to the modern world when it was plundered by British railway engineers beginning in 1856. Needing roadbed ballast for their rails, and having discovered the ancient mound of ruins in Harappā, and being ignorant of its antiquity and archaeological value, the engineers proceeded from 1856 until 1919 to appropriate the mound and its baked clay brick for their railroad. The East Indian Railway from Karachi to Lahore was completed with the help of these bricks and today trains still "rumble over a hundred miles of line laid on a secure foundation of third millennium brick bats."[30] In the process of building the railroad and dismantling the ruins of Harappā many antiquities were discovered, but their significance was not immediately apparent.

It was not until excavations were begun in earnest in 1921 at Harappā by the Indian archaeologist Bahadur Daya Ram Sahni, and at Harappā's sister city of Mohenjodaro in 1922 by R. D. Banerji, that the

---

*The other great river cultures were: The Nile River culture of Ancient Egypt (beginning about 3500 B.C.E.), Yellow River (Huang-Ho) culture (beginning about 2500 B.C.E.), and the Mesopotamian River culture (beginning about 3600 B.C.E.).

full extent of the Indus civilization began to be known. Then, from 1922 to 1927, the government of India authorized the Director General of Archaeology, Sir John Marshall, to proceed with extensive excavations at Mohenjodaro. Working with as many as 1200 laborers, seven levels of the city of Mohenjodaro (and, later, two more) were uncovered. Subsequently, some thirty different excavation campaigns conducted by Europeans, Indians, Pakistanis, and Americans have gone further in uncovering, cataloging, and preserving the discoveries at both Mohenjodaro and Harappā; but nothing in the later diggings can quite compare with the initial archaeological work at Mohenjodaro from 1922 to 1927 under the direction of Marshall.

The two major cities of the Harappān civilization were both constructed according to the same general plan, that is, a city proper, with its avenues laid out in a grid-like pattern of straight streets intersecting at right angles with other streets and alleys and lanes, fronted by plain, thick, brick-walled houses of two to three stories; several hundred feet to the west of each city lay a fortified high-walled citadel or acropolis. Let me concentrate in what follows on the city of Mohenjodaro, remembering that what is said of it could, in most instances, be said of Harappā as well.

Mohenjodaro consists of two large mounds separated by a wide 500-foot gully. The western mound, the citadel, rises some forty feet above the flood plain. To the east of this acropolis stands the city proper. Though only about one-third of the site has actually been excavated, the entire city is known to cover an area of about 240 acres within a circumference of some three miles. It is estimated that the population of this city was slightly over 41,000 persons.[31]

The streets of Mohenjodaro range from nine feet to thirty-four feet in width and up to one-half mile in length. Public wells within the city stand near many of the intersections of the streets and the smaller lanes. Probably the most striking and memorable feature of this ancient city is the vast network of sewers and drains that honeycomb the streets and lanes at depths of one to two feet below the surface. These brick-lined sewers and drains carried waste water from the houses into soak pits and filtration jars placed at intervals within and without the city and, through larger culverts, they drained into the Indus River. Mohenjodaro's sewage system, along with other civic amenities to be mentioned below, suggest a civilization of a rather high order. Speaking about this "civilized" civilization of Mohenjodaro, A. D. Pusalker has noted that:

> The careful town-planning, adequate water supply, and efficient drainage system presuppose an advanced state of civic authority. Lamp posts at intervals indicate the existence of street lighting.
>
> There was also a watch and ward system for different quarters, and large caravanserais and public store-houses were provided.
>
> That the sanitation was well looked after is seen from the rubbish heap consisting of broken pottery, ashes and humus found in deep trenches outside the city.[32]

The houses vary from two rooms in the smallest house to thirty and more in the larger ones. One entered the house from the street side where windowless walls several feet thick fronted on the street. The stark, monotonous brick fronts of the houses and the lack of windows in general produced a drab uniformity that reminded Sir John Marshall of a working district in a county of northwest England:

> Anyone walking for the first time through Mohenjodaro might fancy himself surrounded by the ruins of some present day working town of Lancashire. That is the impression produced by the wide expanse of bare red brick structures, devoid of any semblance of ornament, and bearing in every feature the mark of stark utilitarianism.[33]

In these plain houses, the rooms on the first floor open onto an inner court. One such building is typical of the larger houses: The inner court is surrounded by a series of smaller rooms where the servants of the house may have lived; the larger and cooler rooms of the second floor were most likely maintained for the family proper; the kitchen was probably in a sheltered corner of the main floor; baths, but not toilets, were constructed in both the lower and upper stories with built-in drains and wells for their proper maintenance; the stairways were of solid masonry with wooden risers; the roof was flat, wooden, and probably used for sleeping and family gatherings: This house seems to bespeak wealth, comfort, and security.

Burnt brick was used everywhere throughout all of the cities, from the walls and the foundations, to the streets and fortifications. This brick together with the general plan of the streets, lanes, wells, walls, and houses indicate that the civilization was, indeed, rich and flourishing. Ernest Mackay has commented:

> The fact that the city was built of burnt brick argues that those who lived within it were a prosperous people. Burnt brick is an expensive commodity. It requires a large amount of fuel to burn it and the wastage due to overfiring, warping and cracking is very great.[34]

The high-walled acropolis mound that lay to the west of the city of Mohenjodaro has been excavated and found to contain, among many other structures, a marvelous brick-lined, bituminous, water-proofed pool or bath measuring some eight feet deep by thirty-nine feet by twenty-three feet. The larger buildings surrounding this bath may have been temples, and the smaller ones may have been private rooms used for prayer, study, meditation, or ritual cleansing. In addition, this walled citadel also contained a number of other buildings including assembly halls and a granary, all of which served to turn the acropolis itself into a kind of religious and civic sanctuary. It is believed that the orderly life of the city, its planning, its arts, religion, trade, and economy may have been directed and controlled from this lofty center.

Religion, Lord Śiva, and Bhakti Yoga

The Indus civilization produced a number of memorable and outstanding works of art. They include a seven-inch high steatite bust of a bearded man (see Figure 1; all figures are in Appendix B) regarded by many Indologists (for no very good reason) as a priest of the culture; a four-and-a-half-inch bronze figure of an utterly charming, naked "dancing girl" (see Figure 2); several realistic stone sculptures of the human body, and a scattered collection of over 2000 carved and chiseled seals (1200 at Mohenjodaro alone) about one inch square, made of steatite, faience, ivory, and pottery (see Figure 3). What we know about the daily life and the personal life of the Harappāns can be discovered from the carved pictures on the faces of these small seals.

Several of the seals depict a man seated cross-legged in the style that came much later to be associated with the "lotus posture" of yogis in meditation (see Figure 4). In several of these seals the figure bears an erect penis, indicating that it may have served some kind of fertility function (see Figure 5). Another of these "yogis" (see Figure 6) gives very strong support to the hypothesis that what we are looking at is the first appearance of that being later to be identified as the Hindu God Śiva. Figure 6 shows a man seated in lotus-posture, hands resting on knees (part of the seal is destroyed), heels together (Śiva is the Lord of yogis), surrounded by several wild animals (Śiva is called "*paśupati,*" the Lord of animals), notably the tiger, wearing a tiger mask with a tiger skin over his body (Śiva is closely identified with the tiger), surmounted by a horned headdress (which Lord Śiva also wears in Hindu depictions of this God), bearing an erect penis (Śiva, of all the Hindu Gods, is especially identified with the erect phallus or liṅgam; India is today famous for its thousands of liṅgas consecrated in loving devotion to Lord Śiva, the third member of the Hindu trinity (See Figures 14 and 15). For these and other reasons we may tentatively conclude that the God Śiva is a deity borrowed by the later Hindus from the Harappāns.

Evidence from the seals and potsherds would seem to support the view that the Harappāns were either worshippers of trees or of beings or Gods identified with trees or, most likely, both. At least one species of tree, classifiable from the seals and sherds as the *aśvattha,* pipal or fig, tree is still regarded as sacred by Hindus.[35] Speaking of this tree and the religion of the Harappāns, S. R. Rao has stated:

> Tree-worship was an important cult in the Indus Valley as well as Gujarat, for several seals depicting the pipal (*Ficus religiosa*) sacred to the Hindus and Buddhists alike have been found at Harappān sites.[36]

Many of the Indus seals depict worshippers placing offerings at what appears to be the fig tree (see Figures 7 and 8). Other seals depict a man in the tree with devotees around the base of the trunk; and still others depict the man or tree-God in the tree alone (see Figure 9).

The most remarkable evidence that we have, however, for the claim that we are, indeed, looking at both the origin of the God Śiva and at the origin of bhakti yoga comes from the last set of seals. The chief figures in these seals, to whom so many other figures are kneeling, seem to be not only identified with the fig tree, as above, but they now seem to be emerging from it while kneeling suppliants pay them attention and honor (see Figures 7 through 10). Further, these honored figures seem to be merged with the sacred tree itself (see Figures 11, 12, and 13). Finally, these latter seals might be compared with two more recent (first century B.C.E. and thirteenth century C.E.) Hindu sculptures, depictions of the liṅgam as Lord Śiva emerges from it (see Figures 14 and 15). The evidence for the origins of Lord Śiva as well as of bhakti yoga in the Indus civilization seems, on the evidence, compelling.[37]

The Harappān script, as yet undeciphered, is found in curious characters across the tops of most of the seals while below the script are depicted animals, real and imaginary, Gods and men, domestic, sailing and hunting scenes, scenes of religious worship, as we have seen, and so on. In fact, practically all that we know of these ancient people comes from their seals. The undeciphered language of the Harappāns, composed of some 270 characters, has baffled Indologists thus far and proves to be but one more unsolved mystery in the investigation of these ancient people.

Civicide: The Decline and Fall of the Harappāns

Sometime after 1900 B.C.E. a steady and devastating decline began in the two major cities of the Indus civilization. A number of theories have been advanced to explain this decline. They range from Ernest Mackay's cautious but limited suggestion regarding the physical buildings of Mohenjodaro: "The chief cause of the gradual destruction of the buildings of Mohenjodaro has been the action of salt;"[38] to the more sophisticated reasons offered by A. D. Pusalker to explain the decline of the entire civilization: "The progressive desiccation of the lower Indus Valley was the main cause of the evacuation of the Indus Cities."[39] But Mackay's explanation cannot account for the decline of a civilization: Buildings can be repaired. And Pusalker's explanation is rendered somewhat inconsistent when, after stating that desiccation was the cause of the cities' evacuation, he goes on to hold that the danger of floods "was certainly responsible for the evacuation of Mohenjo-daro."[40] It is difficult to see how both desiccation and flooding can be the main causes of the same phenomenon, the evacuation of Mohenjodaro. Pusalker continues his discussion by admitting: "The Indus floods, however, cannot account entirely for the desertion of the Indus settlements, though possibly climatic changes were an important reason."[41] He concludes by suggesting yet a third cause, following the desiccation and flooding: "It is probable that these rich, unguarded cities, with their unwarlike mercantile population, were sacked by invading tribes, some of whom may have been Āryans."[42]

From all the welter of theories and hypotheses that attempt to account for the fall of the Harappān civilization there are three hypotheses worth considering. They are, first, that the culture was destroyed by external human forces; second, that it was destroyed by external natural forces; and third, that it was destroyed by internal human forces.

The first theory attempts to account for the decline and abandonment of the Indus cities by claiming that external human forces, either the Āryans that Pusalker mentioned or certain unnamed non-Āryan people from the surrounding hills, attacked and sacked the cities. The best evidence for the Āryan invasion theory comes from the digs at Mohenjodaro, and from the Āryans themselves, i.e., from their sacred Vedic texts. At Mohenjodaro in the 1920s archaeologists found six groups of some forty human skeletons left unburied where they had either fallen or been struck down, giving apparent and dramatic confirmation to the theory of an invasion and massacre.

This theory has been attacked by George F. Dales in his brief article, "The Decline of the Harappāns," in which he states:

> For one thing, no one has any exact knowledge of the date when the Āryans first entered the Indus Valley area; they have not yet been identified archaeologically. For another, the sole (and trivial) purpose served by the invasion hypothesis is to explain the demise of Harappān civilization.[43]

But despite what Dales says, the invasion hypothesis does explain another set of data, namely, the references in the Āryan sacred texts, the *Vedas,* to cities and persons that can be easily identified as the dark-skinned Harappāns of the walled fortresses.[44] Thus one of these compositions, the *Ṛg Veda,* abounds with references to the "black one," that is, the "*dasyus*" ("demons") and "*dasas*" ("savages") who live in the walled citadels that are destroyed by Lord Indra *Puraṃdara* ("the fort-destroyer"):

> As an axe fells the tree so he slew Vṛtra [a "barrier" and a demon], He broke down the enclosures [dams or walls] and dug out the rivers. He split the mountains like a new made pitcher.[45]

And here is another quite random reference:

> the slayer of Vṛtra split the Dasyu fortresses which carried the black inhabitants in their wombs.[46]

And finally there is this:

> Let our true God subdue the hostile rabble: let not those whose God is the phallus [*śiśna-deva*] come near our sacred worship.[47]

The significant question should not be, At what exact time did the Āryans enter the Indus Valley? We believe that they may have begun to enter as early as 1800 B.C.E., at about the same time that the Harappān civilization was either dying or already dead. Rather the significant question should be, If the Āryans invaded the Indus Valley then why didn't the Harappāns stop them?

The second theory that attempts to account for the decline and abandonment of the Indus cities, particularly Mohenjodaro, is advanced by both George F. Dales[48] and Sir Mortimer Wheeler. Essentially, this second theory argues that certain external natural forces, rather than external human forces, brought an end to the cities. These natural forces took the form of catastrophic geological disturbances somewhere south of Mohenjodaro. These disturbances threw up natural rock fault dams that caused marshing and ponding upstream to Mohenjodaro, thereby flooding the city. These floods either caused the evacuation of Mohenjodaro and the southern sites of the civilization, as Dales maintains, or it brought about a problem in internal morale within the city itself as Wheeler maintains:

> From whatever cause, the intermittent floods at Mohenjo-daro . . . no doubt helped, by a process of attrition, to wear down the morale of the inhabitants, and may have contributed to the progressive

> deterioration which has long been recognized in their civic standards.[49]

But if such geologic faulting and damming did occur, then a compelling question naturally arises: Why didn't the Harappāns break the dams? for they had the technology, as well as the urgent need, to put that technology into operation.

The third theory that attempts to account for the decline and abandonment of the Indus cities, particularly the fall of Mohenjodaro, argues that neither external human forces nor external natural forces are to blame for the fall of the Harappān culture. Rather that fall was brought about by internal human forces. The internal human forces that we can identify from the ruins are urban pollution, overpopulation, and a systematic ravaging of the natural environment. There is, for example, a striking difference in the quality of life between the earlier (deeper) and the more recent (uppermost) archaeological levels of excavation at Mohenjodaro. At the earlier levels, as mentioned previously, we find all of the civic and social characteristics of a well-planned, well-developed, and well-run municipality. The streets were wide, spacious, and, though monotonously plain and unexciting, not without a certain clean and aesthetic attractiveness. The houses were large, open, simply, and modestly decorated, and not unattractive. The sewer system, the rather sophisticated grain storage facilities, and the evidence of the building and trade professions, all bespeak a growing, flourishing, healthy, and handsome city, inhabited by an industrious, energetic, and technologically capable people. And thus things remained for several hundred years.

Then, the excavations indicate, as time passed, the population swelled and spilled out and over the older well-established limits. According to Wheeler, and it is evident from the diggings, new but badly made houses were hastily fashioned on the ruins of the older ones.

> Houses . . . were increasingly shoddier in construction, increasingly carved up into warrens for a swarming lower-grade population. . . . Economic decline is everywhere apparent. . . .[50]

The rooms of the older houses were divided and partitioned, the streets were narrowed while the magnificent and capacious gridiron pattern of old was broken as smaller slum-like tenements filled in the spaces to accommodate the burgeoning population. Mohenjodaro, and with it probably the Harappān culture in general, began to die. The Harappāns became progressively incapable of coping with their various and devastating internal problems of civic pollution, growing slums, the overgrazing, the plundering of the forests to provide the fuel for the millions of bricks used in the city's building and rebuilding, together with the rampant population and the uncontrollable and unpredictable vagaries of nature: All of this surely made the culture ripe for flooding, invasion, and conquest, if, indeed, there was anything left to flood, invade, or conquer.

The three hypothetical causes of the decline and fall of the Harappān civilization are undoubtedly related. The picture that emerges is that of a once energetic, ambitious, conscientious, and dedicated people finally overcome, overthrown, and conquered, not by foreign invaders or by floods, but by themselves. The Āryans were not responsible, the river was not responsible; the major cause of the decline and death of Mohenjodaro and the Harappān civilization, which made the two previous causes operable, probably lay within the civilization's own people. For, ironically enough, they seem to have possessed the technology as well as the wisdom to solve both of their external problems. But some strange myopia prevented them from recognizing that the cause of their own decline and fall was to lie within the city walls, among the inhabitants, in the hearts of the citizens themselves. The Indus Valley civilization, its magnificent cities, its arts and crafts, its language and government, its technology and collective wisdom passed suddenly and terribly from the pages of history through an act that is, perhaps, best described as "civicide."[51]

The Rx for Liberation from Suffering: The Harappāns

There is not enough information available to reconstruct fully the religion of the Harappāns. Applying our heuristic schema, the Rx for liberation from suffering, to what we do know, would lead, however, to the following conjectures.

The Problems

The problems that the Harappāns faced may have been a *concern* with life after death coupled with an *anxiety* over survival and prosperity in this life. We know that many of their dead were buried with common possessions, for example, bowls, pots, beads, ornaments, and weapons, which may indicate a belief in, and a concern for, a life after death. We also know from the seals that there may have been considerable anxiety regarding the powers and "Gods" of trees, vegetation, and fertility.

The Causes

The causes of the concern about life after death as well as the anxiety over survival in this life are probably connected to the uncontrollability of hostile forces and powers in nature.

The Solution

The solution to the problems of concern over the next life and anxiety over this one probably lay in controlling those hostile forces that prevent a better life in the next birth and a prosperous life now.

The Ways

The ways to the solution may have involved propitiation of, worship of, or adoration of, either the liṅgam or certain deities associated with vegetation cults including the worship of trees or proto-yogis or proto-Śivas who sit cross-legged on raised platforms and emerge from fig trees in order to be worshipped. If this is so, then we have here the origin of devotional, or bhakti, yoga in India.

The Guiding Principle or Person

The Principle or Person that would guarantee that following the ways would lead to a solution of the problem by attacking the causes are, unfortunately, not known. However, if the Harappāns were worshippers of trees and of Gods of fertility and vegetation, then we might conjecture that the power to solve the problem of suffering lay in nature and that the guaranteeing or guiding Principle or Person was a power in the natural world.

The results of our enquiry into the Harappān religion is admittedly conjectural, but they would look like Table 2.1.

Table 2.1 **The Rx for Liberation from Suffering: The Harappāns**

Problem:	Suffering as the concern about life after death and anxiety over survival and prosperity in this life
Cause:	The realization that certain external and natural forces were not controllable
Solution:	Achieving a better life after death and attaining the power over those threatening forces in this life
Ways:	Propitiation through bhakti yoga of Gods and forces associated with life, trees, vegetation, fertility, survival and prosperity
Guiding Principle or Person:	Unknown, though possibly associated with some power or personal God in nature

Summary

The importance of the Harappāns and the Indus Valley civilization to Hinduism lies in the fact that many elements in that later religion may be traceable, not to the Āryans, but to the Harappāns. Thus the Harappān religious contribution to Hinduism may include such practices as phallic worship, meditational and bhakti yogas, worship of the Great Mother (whose status may be similar to that of the Mother Goddess and *magna mater* of Mesopotamia and the ancient Mediterranean religions of the same period), cults of trees, waters, and animals, beliefs in transmigration and liberation, together with a host of indigenous village deities, demons, ghosts, and spirits.[52]

We turn next to the second foundation of Hinduism: Brahminism and the *Vedas.*

The *Vedas* (1500-900 B.C.E.): Brahminism (The Way of Action)

The *Vedas* ("veda" is from the Sanskrit root *vid,* "to know," hence the *Vedas* are the books of knowledge) are said to contain all possible knowledge about man and the Gods. The tradition says that the *Vedas* were revealed to certain ṛṣis or seers who *heard* these śruti. The śruti include the following: The collection of hymns called the *Vedas;* the *Brāhmaṇas* or commentaries on these hymns; the *Āraṇyakas* or forest treatises, which are recitations to be chanted by those ṛṣis or celibates who lived a retired and solitary life in the forest; and, finally, it includes the dozens of *Upaniṣads,* which are the philosophical speculations on the Vedic hymns.

These Vedic hymns, in turn, fall into four groups or books: First, the *Ṛg Veda,* which is a collection of the earliest Āryan hymns, and the *Veda* to which we shall be devoting all of our labors shortly; the *Sāma Veda,* a collection of *Ṛg Veda* verses arranged for liturgical purposes; the *Yajur Veda,* a collection of sacrificial formula which were meant to be employed in the Vedic sacrifice; and, finally, the *Atharva Veda,* the most recent of the *Vedas,* composed sometime between 800 to 500 B.C.E. and long after the Āryan invaders had settled in India. This latter *Veda* is a collection of spells and incantations, and white and black magical formulas, for securing all sorts of goals and goods. Here, for example, is a grisly *Atharva* charm for depriving an enemy, a man, of his virility:

> As the best of the plants thou art reputed, O herb [The priest is probably holding the plant in his hand while chanting this curse]: turn this man for me to-day into a eunuch that wears his hair dressed!
>
> Turn him into a eunuch that wears his hair dressed, and into one that wears a hood! Then Indra with a pair of stones shall break his testicles both!
>
> O eunuch, into a eunuch thee have I turned; O castrate, into a castrate thee have I turned; O weakling, into a weakling thee have I turned! A hood upon his head, and a hair-net do we place.

> The two canals, fashioned by the gods, in which man's power rests, in thy testicles . . . I break them with a club [Here, the plant, which the priest held and which may have resembled the enemy's penis, was probably struck and crushed by a club or a stone].
>
> As women break reeds for a mattress with a stone, thus do I break thy member. . . .[53]

But the *Atharva Veda* also contains cosmological and metaphysical speculations on, *inter alia*, Brahman, the nature of the self, and the One underlying all phenomena, presaging matters more fully developed in the *Upaniṣads*.

The Ṛg Veda

The *Ṛg Veda* mantras or hymns are the oldest and the most philosophical of the four *Vedas*. The *Ṛg Veda* itself is the oldest religious text still in common use in the world today since many of its hymns are chanted by nearly all Hindus the moment they wake in the morning. For example, here is probably the most sacred hymn of all the Vedic hymns, the Gāyatrī prayer to Savitṛ, the Lord of the sun, repeated upon rising by all Hindus and at the start of all religious rites and ceremonies:

> Tat Savitur vareniam
> bhargo devasya dhīmahi
> dhiyo yo naḥ pracodayāt.
>
> Let us consider the shining brilliance
> of Lord Savitṛ that he may
> inspire our hearts.[54]

The religious life of most Hindus today remains focused on this collection of 1028 Sanskrit hymns from the *Ṛg Veda*. The hymns are addressed to the innumerable Gods of heaven and earth and the sky between. The chief deities of the Āryans were Indra, the God of war and the thunderstorm, the most popular God of the Āryans, but a deity utterly ignored by contemporary Hinduism; Agni, the God of fire; Soma, the Lord of the ritual sacrifice at which the intoxicating, but nonalcoholic, drug called "soma" was drunk by the Gods and priests; Yama, the Lord of the dead and the underworld; Āpas, the Lord of waters; Vāyu, the Lord of the wind; and Savitṛ or Sūrya, the Lord of the sun.

The theology of the *Vedas* seems to have evolved from a *polytheism,* wherein many Gods were worshipped, to a *henotheism,* where one God was regarded as supreme over the other Gods for a brief time. This henotheistic supremacy might exist for a particular occasion, such as a sacrifice, or for a longer, but limited, period of time as an individual deity's popularity rose. Hinduism subsequently evolved a kind of *monotheism* in which one God became so popular that the other Gods turned into mere supernumeraries in relation to Him or Her, acting more like angels or messengers of the one supreme God than as full-blown Gods themselves. But the theism of the *Vedas* and of Hinduism is best summarized by the chant: "He is One, but people call Him by many different names."

Varṇa Dharma: The Origin of the Four Classes

The Vedic religion centered around the household fire sacrifice and the public ritual sacrifice. The latter was a ceremony conducted by the priests, or brahmin varṇa, for the warrior and ruling class, the kṣatriya varṇa, or for members of the merchant and propertied class, the vaiśya varṇa; but they were not available to nor conducted for the *śūdra* varṇa, the serving class. These varṇas (the Sanskrit word for "color") were rigidly controlled and strictly regulated by *dharma* (the Sanskrit word for "law"), for the *Ṛg Veda* itself had created the four varṇas. The varṇas are first set forth in a creation story that describes the origin of everything from a gigantic person or Puruṣa. This Puruṣa is sacrificed and divided until the various parts of It become the earth, the sun, the moon, the animals, and so on. Human beings are created from this Puruṣa, as well:

> When they divided Puruṣa into how many portions did they arrange him? What was his mouth? What his arms? What his thighs and feet?

> The brahmin was his mouth; his two arms made the kṣatriya; his two thighs the vaiśya; and from his feet was made the śūdra.[55]

It is easy to see that the varṇa, or class, distinctions are based on occupations. And then as now the brahmin's duty lay in conducting the sacrifice and teaching the sacred knowledge of the *Vedas* to qualified pupils; the kṣatriya managed the ruling and defense of the clan or state; the vaiśya supplied the trade and food that kept the clan alive and materially prosperous; and the śūdra served the other three classes and looked after their menial needs. Abuse of the varṇa dharma may have occurred as with any social system, then or now, and since 1947 the constitution of the Republic of India has made discrimination on the basis of class or caste a crime.

With the Gods and the varṇas behind us, let us look at the sacrifice and the ritual hymns of the *Ṛg Veda* with the Rx for liberation as our guide. Let us try to find out what problems an Āryan or Vedic person might have faced from 1500 to 900 B.C. and why he or she thought the *Vedas,* the sacrifice, the brahmins, and the Gods could help in solving those problems.

The Rx for Liberation from Suffering: The Ṛg Veda

The Problems

Vedic men and women probably faced problems not unlike those faced by men and women today. And in facing those problems they did what many religious men and women do today: They went to God or the Gods for help. For this reason, brahminism, the religion of Vedic man, is not at first glance a difficult religion to understand; the reader may even find a certain sympathy being generated for Vedic man's attempts to come to grips with those problems through the sacrifice, the brahmins, and the Gods.

What were the problems that brahminism was supposed to solve? They are manifold but familiar. One thing Vedic man wanted, we learn from the *Ṛg Veda,* was material goods, i.e., land, cattle, and wealth. This moving hymn is addressed to Prajāpati, the Lord of the universe, as the worshipper praises this God, honors him, presents gifts to him and earnestly prays that Prajāpati will grant his request:

As the Golden Seed he arose in the beginning; when born he was the only Lord of all that existed. He supported the earth and this heaven. What God with our gifts shall we worship?

He who gives breath, who gives strength, who commands that all the Gods obey, whose shadow is life immortal, and the lord of death, as well. What God with our gifts shall we worship?

Who through his greatness has become the sole ruler over those who breathe and those who blink; He who is lord of the two-footed and the four-footed. What God with our gifts shall we worship?

His are, through his greatness, these snowy mountains. His are the ocean and the great river Rasā that surrounds heaven and earth. His are the embracing arms and all the regions he embraces. What God with our gifts shall we worship?

By him are the heavens strong and the earth steadfast, by him the sun and the earth are supported. By him the regions between sun and earth were measured. What God with our gifts shall we worship?

To him the heaven and earth, upheld by his aid, look up, trembling in their hearts, as over them the risen sun shines. What God with our gifts shall we worship?

When the great waters came containing the seed of all within and generating fire, then he sprang forth into being, the one life spirit of the Gods. What God with our gifts shall we worship?

Who through his greatness beheld the waters pregnant with power and generated the sacrifice, he who was the one God beyond all the other Gods. What God with our gifts shall we worship?

> May he not injure us who is earth's father, he of the just laws, heaven's creator, who has brought forth the mighty and shining waters. What God with our gifts shall we worship?
>
> Oh Prajāpati, none other than you embrace all these created beings and you alone. Oh Prajāpati, when we call unto you grant us our hearts' desire. Oh Prajāpati, may we become lords of wealth.[56]

But the lack of wealth and the fear of God's wrath were not the only things about which to be anxious. Another anxiety gnawed at Vedic man. It was the terrible sense of guilt that comes at the thought that a sin may have been committed against the law or the Gods. Appeals expressing this fear were generally directed to Lord Varuṇa, a savior deity, who has the power to forgive sins and prevent the punishment and suffering that would ordinarily follow from them:

> Let me not yet, King Varuṇa, enter into the house of clay: Have mercy, spare me, Mighty Lord.
>
> When, Oh Hurler-of-Stones, I move along tremulous like a swollen goatskin: Have mercy, spare me, Mighty Lord.
>
> Oh bright and powerful God, through want of strength I erred and went astray: Have mercy, spare me, Mighty Lord.
>
> Thirst for more has seized your worshipper though he stood in the midst of water-floods of plenty: Have mercy, spare me, Mighty Lord.
>
> Oh Varuṇa, whatever the offense may be which we as men commit against the heavenly host, when, through carelessness, we violate your laws, punish us not, Oh God, for that iniquity.[57]

The problems that Vedic man faced would seem to come down to these two: First, the fear that he would not have sufficient material goods in this world; and second, because of his sins, the fear that he would not get to heaven when this life was over but that he would be taken to the house of clay, that is, that the earth would be the end of him. The problems for Vedic man, then, encompassed anxieties about his desires for the wealth of this world and the pleasures of the heaven to come.

The Causes

The causes of the anxiety have already been touched on above. Those causes relate to man's disobedience of the eternal Vedic laws and his inattention to the Gods, an inattention that could lead to the Gods' inattention to man. There was a kind of *quid pro quo*, a this for that, in the relation between the Gods and man such that the Gods would nourish man as long as man nourished them. Once that nourishment or attention had been given to the Gods through the sacrifice of cattle and the mysterious and precious soma juice, then wealth or heaven would be granted to man. Here is a portion of a hymn that seeks to correct any neglect of Indra that might have led to the loss of wealth:

> Indra is sovereign Lord of earth and heaven;
> Indra is Lord of waters and of mountains.
> Indra is master of those who prosper and the wise;
> Indra must be invoked for the acquiring and the preserving of wealth.[58]

And here is a hymn to Viṣṇu, a creator deity in the *Vedas,* expressing the sacrificer's heavenly desire along with his earthly anxiety:

> May I attain to that, his well-loved mansion, where men devoted to the Gods are happy....
> Happily would we go to your dwelling places where there are many horned and nimble oxen....[59]

It seems clear, then, that the two problems of gaining wealth and heaven are caused, first, by disobedience of the eternal laws, a disobedience that led, from what we have seen previously, to unforgiven sins that, in turn, fetch one neither wealth nor heaven but only anxiety, malaise, and, eventually, the house of clay; and, second, by neglect of the Gods and the ritual sacrifice.

The Solution

The solution to the two problems obviously lay in securing the power to gain both wealth and heaven.

The Ways

The ways to wealth and heaven lay in the activity of propitiating the Gods and having one's sins properly erased. Here is another hymn to Varuṇa detailing one of those ways:

> Truly wise are all creatures through the greatness of him who pushed earth and spacious heaven apart, who sent aloft the dome of the sky, who put the sun on its double journey, above and below the earth, and who then spread the earth before him.
>
> With my heart I ponder the question, How may Varuṇa and I be united? What gift of mine will he accept without anger? When may I look and find him gracious?

But then the anxiety returns as the sinner, sounding like an *Old Testament* Job, ponders his crimes, known and unknown, conscious and unconscious:

> Anxious to know my sin I question others; Oh Varuṇa, I seek the wise and I question them. And this self-same answer all the sages give back to me: surely Lord Varuṇa is angry with you.
>
> Oh Varuṇa, what has been my chief transgression that you would thus slay the friend who hymns your praises? Oh unconquerable Lord, do but tell me and quickly, sinless, will I approach you with my homage.
>
> Free us from sins committed by our fathers, as well as those that we ourselves have committed....

And what are the causes of those sins?

> It was not my own will that betrayed me, but thoughtlessness, Oh Varuṇa, wine, dice and anger. The old and stronger are always near at hand to lead the young and weaker astray, and even gentle sleep does not remove all evil doing.

So, now, what is to be done?

> As a slave may I render service to my bounteous Lord. May I be free from sin and serve the God inclined to anger. This noble Lord gives wisdom to the ignorant and leads the wise man to riches.

And the hymn and the sinner conclude:

> Oh Lord Varuṇa, may my hymn of praise come to rest in your heart. With your blessings may all go well with us forever.[60]

The ways to the solution of the problem of suffering entail cleansing oneself of sins committed against the laws of man and God, making oneself contrite and penitent, and proclaiming all of this through a properly conducted sacrifice. Therefore, the principal way to gain the forgiveness of the Gods lay in seeing to it that the sacrifice, to whomever directed, was properly conducted. Two kinds of sacrifice seem to have been available to Vedic man: First, the *śrauta* or "solemn" ritual, which used three fires and employed several (as many as sixteen) priests; second, the *gṛhya* or "domestic" or "nonsolemn" ritual, which used only the household fire and one priest, the *purohita*.[61] The sacrifice, properly carried out by the brahmins, could assure Vedic man of both wealth and forgiveness of sins, that is, it could assure him of happiness in this world and the next.

This meant, of course, that the power of the brahmins was enormous since they alone held the keys to the wealth of earth and the pleasures of heaven. The way to wealth and heaven lay then in pleasing the priests as much as the Gods, and it is probably true that brahminism became, as a consequence, a religion for the few, administered and controlled by a powerful brahmin class.

The Guiding Principle and Person

Ṛta

The Principle that appears to guarantee that following the ways will lead to liberation from suffering, i.e., to wealth and to heaven, is called *Ṛta,* ("the course of things") in the *Ṛg Veda*. Ṛta is a principle of cosmic order with powers to keep everything in their proper physical and moral places in the universe. If anything gets out of place, physically or morally, then it is Ṛta's task to put things back in place. Ṛta functions as a sort of Vedic version of the Newtonian law of gravity, on the one hand, and a sort of Upaniṣadic law of karma, on the other. Thus, if you drop this book in midair, then it will fall. Why? Because to put a book in midair, unsupported by anything, is to do a physical injustice to the universe and to the orderly way of things. So, Ṛta takes notice of this physical injustice and corrects it by bringing the book down to its proper, i.e., just and fair, place, the ground, thereby restoring order to the physical universe. If you kill someone, then you will be punished. Why? Because to kill someone is to do a moral injustice to the universe. So, Ṛta notices this moral injustice and corrects it by bringing punishment on the sinner, thereby restoring order to the moral universe.

Ṛta is also personified as a deity in the *Ṛg Veda*. In the following hymn a priest praises Ṛta, hoping thereby to raise his fee for the sacrifice, a payment in cows:

> Ṛta has varied food that gives strength; the thought of Ṛta
> removes transgressions.
>
> The hymns in praise of Ṛta, arousing and glowing, have opened
> the deaf ears of the living.
>
> Firmly grounded are Ṛta's foundations: in its fair form there are
> many splendid beauties;
>
> By holy Ṛta long-lasting food is brought to us; by holy Ṛta the
> cows are brought to pay us for the sacrifice.

> Fixing Ṛta, Indra now upholds it; swiftly moves the might of Ṛta and wins the rewards.
>
> To Ṛta belongs the vast deep earth and heaven, the cows of the sacrifice, to Ṛta they render the milk.[62]

Varuṇa

But Ṛta vies in power with Gods such as Varuṇa who seems to have had the ability to counter the corrections and pay-offs of Ṛta. When the sinner, who deserves punishment, pleads with Varuṇa, he does it expecting that the pay-off will be permanently put-off:

> Varuṇa, strike us not with those dread weapons which at your bidding wound the sinner. Let us not pass from the light into exile.
>
> Oh mighty Varuṇa, now and hereafter, even as of old, will we speak forth our worship. For in yourself, invincible God, your unchangeable statutes are fixed as if carved in rock.[63]

So it is a question of what or who is to have the Power. Can Varuṇa counter the laws relating to the just punishment of sinners as prescribed by Ṛta? Then Varuṇa has the sovereignty. Or is Ṛta invincible, controlling even Varuṇa? Then Ṛta has the sovereignty. The question regarding sovereignty is moot since a development occurred in the post-Vedic period (ca. 800 B.C.E.) and immediately prior to the Upaniṣadic period that altered the entire question of sovereignty, namely, the evolution of the concept of Brahman. Before turning to that matter, refer to Table 2.2 for a summary of the results of our inquiry thus far.

Table 2.2 The Rx for Liberation from Suffering: The *Vedas*

Problems:	**Anxiety about getting wealth in this world and heaven in the next**
Causes:	**Disobedience and neglect of the eternal laws and the ritual sacrifice**
Solution:	**Achieving the power to obtain wealth and heaven**
Ways:	**Leading a moral life and paying attention to the Gods through prayer and sacrifice, i.e., through the way of action in this world**
Guiding Principle or Person:	Ṛta and Varuṇa

Transition to the Upaniṣads

The power of the priests, as we have noted, was enormous. They knew the prescription to the liberation from suffering, that is, they knew what ailed their patients and they had the catholicon for the cure. But then something happened in the immediate post-Vedic period that was to change brahminism in a most extraordinary manner from a polytheistic or henotheistic religion into a kind of ritual atheism.

Consider the ordinary route from problem to solution in the brahmin's attempt to help a patron. It may have gone something like this: The patron, i.e., the patient, the sinner, or the petitioner, desires a cure for his suffering. He goes to the brahmin with his problem. The brahmin diagnoses the suffering or knows how to cure it. He conducts the ritual sacrifice by calling the Gods to the feast where he charms and flatters them, gets their attention, feeds them and then presents the petition of his patron, a petition for wealth, forgiveness, victory in battle, or the right to enter heaven and avoid obliteration in the house of clay (there was no clear concept of hell for Vedic man). That is *ordinary* brahminism.

But then the priests made two momentous discoveries that transformed ordinary brahminism into *extraordinary* brahminism: First, they discovered that the holy chantings of the sacrifice could compel the Gods to attend the sacrifice and to do the bidding of the priests.

Ritual sacrifice turned into ritual compulsion. Franklin Edgerton comments on this new discovery:

> At first merely a means of gratification and propitiation of the gods [ordinary brahminism], the sacrifice gradually became an end in itself, and finally, in the period succeeding the hymns of the Rig Veda, the gods became supernumeraries. The now all-important sacrifices no longer persuaded, but compelled them to do what the sacrificer desired; or else, at times, the sacrifice produced the desired result immediately, without any participation whatsoever on the part of the gods [extraordinary brahminism].[64]

Second, they discovered that they didn't need the Gods at all but only their Power. With that Power one could get the wealth, the forgiveness, victory, and heaven. The Power was what was important, after all, and not the Gods. They now realized that this Power was contained in the sacrificial chant that called the Gods to the sacrifice, such that whoever knew the chant, possessed the Power. The name for this hymn or chant was "brahman," and the name "brahman" initially meant any sacred or magical formula. As time passed, "brahman" came to be identified, not with the words or chants that conjured up the Gods and their Power, but with the Power itself. Edgerton continues:

> The spoken word had a mysterious, supernatural power; it contained within itself the essence of the thing denoted. To "know the name" of anything was to control the thing. The *word* means wisdom, knowledge; and knowledge . . . was (magic) power. So *brahman*, the "holy word," soon came to mean the mystic power inherent in the holy word.[65]

To the brahmin who knew the holy word "brahman," then, the Holy Power, "Brahman," was his as well: "All human desires and aspirations were accessible to him who mastered It."[66]

Extraordinary brahminism gave enormous power and influence to the priests. But this concentration of power and influence was to prove their undoing in the end as it led to a conceptual revolution against brahminism and a religious reformation.

Summary

As brahminism, the religion of the *Vedas,* evolved from ordinary brahminism (the religion that centered exclusively around a priestly controlled ritual sacrifice) to extraordinary brahminism (the religion that centered around Power), it became a religion of the few, that is, a religion for those who could afford the sometimes enormous fees charged by the brahmins and necessitated by the śrauta sacrifices. The religion became Power oriented, excessively ritualistic, priest-dominated, and aristocratic. Such a religion tended to exclude the masses of the people since the ritual sacrifice was for the use only of the three highest varṇas, the brahmins, the kṣatriyas, and the vaiśyas, and it was not for the use of śūdras, outcastes, and noncastes. Thus even though the gṛhya or household sacrifices were available, the poor and less fortunate may have found in brahminism cold comfort for the problems that they faced in their anxiety about this life and the life to come.

Brahminism was ripe for change and change in one form came with the philosophic and religious revolution of the *Upaniṣads* as more attention came to be focused on Brahman, the Holy Power. It was possible, the *Upaniṣads* seemed to say, for *anyone* who was properly qualified and who practiced the right kind of discipline to know Brahman and thereby possess the Power of Brahman. The similarities to the Protestant Reformation of the sixteenth century seem rather strong, as we shall see.

The *Upaniṣads* (800-200 B.C.E.): Brahmanism (The Way of Knowledge)

The *Upaniṣads* (from *upa,* "near," *ni,* "down," *sad,* "to sit," i.e., "upaniṣad" means "to sit down near," so close, in fact, that the teacher could whisper in your ear; thus the *Upaniṣads* are often called "the secret teachings" of Hinduism) constitute the philosophical commentaries on the *Vedas*. In making those commentaries, however, they go far beyond the matters contained in the *Vedas* and in brahminism. In one sense the *Upaniṣads* are a response to both the exclusiveness of ordinary brahminism and the priestly domination of extraordinary brahminism. In another sense they are a natural outgrowth and evolution of both as attention came to be focused on

Brahman and on the locus of Brahman among Indians seeking solutions to the problem of the liberation from suffering. The stage was set for seeking solutions not by turning outwardly to the Gods, whether with priestly help and sacrifices or not, but by turning within oneself to where Brahman resides.

In order to illustrate this break with the exclusivity of ordinary brahminism and the priestly domination of extraordinary brahminism, consider the following story. It is about a young boy, the son of a sudra mother and an unknown father, a boy who wants to become a student of sacred knowledge. The question that the story raises is this: Is one a brahmin by virtue of birth or by virtue of one's behavior?

> Once upon a time Satyakāma Jābāla addressed his mother Jabālā: "Madam! I desire to live the life of a student of sacred knowledge. Of what family am I?"
>
> Then she said to him: "I do not know this, my son, of what family you are. In my youth, when I went about a great deal serving as a maid, I got you. So I do not know of what family you are. However, I am Jabālā by name; you are Satyakāma by name. So you may speak of yourself as Satyakāma Jābāla."
>
> Then he went to Hāridrumata Gautama, and said: "I will live the life of a student of sacred knowledge. I will become a pupil of yours, sir."
>
> To him Hāridrumata then said: "Of what family are you, young man?" Then Satyakāma replied: "I do not know this, sir, of what family I am. I asked my mother and she answered me: 'In my youth, when I went about a great deal serving as a maid, I got you. So I do not know this, of what family you are. However, I am Jabālā by name; you are Satyakāma by name.' So I am Satyakāma Jābāla, sir."
>
> To him Hāridrumata then said: "Only a brahmin would be able to explain thus. Bring the fuel, young man. I will receive you as a pupil. You have not deviated from the truth."[67]

If behavior does indeed determine varṇa then two puzzling questions would appear to follow for contemporary Hinduism. First, Mohandas Gandhi and A. C. Bhaktivedanta were both born vaiśyas; yet Gandhi behaved like a kṣatriya all of his life, becoming a lawyer, a political leader, and a statesman; and Bhaktivedanta, while behaving like a tradesman and businessman for much of his life, exhibited toward the end certain brahmin behaviors, sacrificing and teaching according to the sacred texts of Hinduism. So, to which varṇas did they really belong? Second, if one takes Hāridrumata's observation seriously then one could in a single lifetime span all of the possible behaviors of the varṇas, serving today in menial tasks, in business tomorrow, in the army the day after, and teaching the sacred texts the day following, sliding back and forth between consistent and inconsistent varṇa behaviors. So, to which varṇa would such a slider belong given such a behavioral jumble? The problem remains: Either varṇa is as varṇa does or varṇa does as varṇa is.

Tiger Natures: Tat Tvam Asi

The conceptual revolution brought about in India by the Rx for liberation of the *Upaniṣads* coincides with the worldwide revolution in philosophy from the sixth through the fourth centuries B.C. in Greece with Parmenides, Heraclitus, Democritus, Protagoras, Socrates, Plato, and Aristotle; in China with Confucius, Lao Tzu, and Chuang Tzu; and in India with the Carvaka materialists, the Jains, and the Buddhists. It is a period fraught with military ventures, rapid increases in population, and large displacements of people and institutions, together with the introduction of revolutionary ideas and doctrines in philosophy, religion, sociology, and economics. India itself and the Ganges River Valley, in particular, were to be testing grounds for many ideological changes and in no place is the sudden displacement of ideas more obvious than in the *Upaniṣads.* Let us look at this revolution in ideas by considering the following Indian story which every Hindu child knows and which captures the spirit of the *Upaniṣads* in a most unique way.

> Once upon a time a tigress and her newly born cub were set upon by hunters in the jungle and the mother was killed. The cub, too small to be detected by the hunters, lay concealed and, after the

hunters had gone, it wandered about the forest bawling for its mother. Suddenly, it came upon a large meadow where a flock of sheep were grazing. The tiger cub, hungry from its exertions, tottered to one of the nursing and startled ewes who eventually let it suckle. And so the cub settled down with the sheep and in time grew fat and sheepish. It learned to bleat after a fashion, to crop grass, and to eat by day and to sleep by night. Several years passed in this way when one day matters took a sudden and unexpected turn. From out of the jungle and into the flock of sheep ran a full-grown, powerful tiger. The flock of sheep scattered wildly but the cub, now a strong youth, stood his ground. The older tiger, seeing him, approached and gazed at his younger counterpart who had sprigs of green grass protruding from his mouth.

"Who are you?" the youngster asked.

"Who are you? is the real question," the older tiger demanded.

"I'm a sheep," the former replied.

"A sheep, indeed!" snorted the other. Whereupon the cub gave out a sheep-like-tiger-like "Baaah," seriously startling the older tiger. With that the latter grabbed the youngster by the scruff of the neck and dragged him down to a cool, clear pond close by.

"There! Look there! What do you see in the water?"

"My reflection. My face."

"Is it a sheep's face? Look again!"

Bewildered the cub gazed at the striped and whiskered face which he had seen before hundreds of times in the same pool.

"Now who are you?" the older tiger demanded. "Are you a sheep or are you like me?"

Confused, and full of doubts, the youth replied, "I don't know. I thought I was a sheep."

With that the older tiger trotted off, caught and killed one of the sheep in the flock. He dragged the carcass back to where the perplexed cub crouched, gazing at his tiger-like face in the still waters.

"Here, taste this!" shouted the older tiger; and with that, thrust the youth's muzzle into the warm blood of the freshly killed sheep. "Now who are you?"

The first taste of blood now awakened the natural instincts and dormant wisdom of the cub. Rising from his haunches over the kill, he roared forth his reply, "I'm a tiger!!"

With that the two tigers bounded off into the jungle to hunt.

The story of the tiger cub who discovered who he really was (a bit gruesome, perhaps, with a touch of ingratitude on the part of the cub in relation to the sheep who had raised a lost orphan) is used by Upaniṣadic philosophers to illustrate the central point of the *Upaniṣads* or the Vedānta ("the end," *anta,* "of the *Vedas*"), that is, the philosophical commentaries on the *Vedas:* The discovery of Who we really are constitutes liberation or mokṣa.

The story also illustrates the teaching relationship that exists between a master or guru, the older tiger, and the pupil or *śiṣya,* the cub. In Vedāntic terms, the cub is caught up in the ignorance, avidyā, of his true Self; "I'm a sheep," he says. The guru forces him to look at himself and, for the first time, as a result of this encounter with himself, doubts arise as to his real nature. "I don't know," he says, "I thought I was a sheep." As the teaching continues, he is presented with the blood of the dead sheep. Suddenly his instincts revive and he is awakened to his true nature. The guru has led his śiṣya to liberation: The pupil knows Who he is.

The Vedānta teaching is concerned with this discovery of the real Self, and the *Upaniṣads* teach that that Self is the same in all beings. This Self, "Ātman" in Sanskrit, is Brahman, now called "the Holy Power of the universe," and the discovery of this identity between the Self and that Power leads to mokṣa. It is the guru's task to bring his śiṣya to this realization and to help him to understand Who he is.

Consider this parable from the *Chāndogya Upaniṣad.* In the sixth chapter of this second oldest *Upaniṣad* (ca. 750 B.C.E.) we find a twelve-year-old śiṣya named Śvetaketu being sent by his father, Uddālaka, to study the science of sacred knowledge, the *Vedas,* with a guru. The youth returns twelve years later, at the age of twenty-four, all puffed up with the learning he has received (it looks like a wasted twelve years from a *Vedānta* point of view). Uddālaka then questions Śvetaketu about what he has learned, and in the process points up the youth's unrestrained ignorance; the youth, in effect, still thinks that he's a sheep, and so the teacher begins leading him to the still waters of knowledge. This *Upaniṣad* offers us a fine glimpse of the guru-śiṣya relationship as well as giving us some insight into what really matters as far as the *Upaniṣads* are concerned. Here, then, is the parable of the rivers:

"All these rivers flow, my son, the eastern toward the east, the western toward the west. But they really flow from the ocean and then back to the ocean, once again. Flowing, they become the ocean itself, and becoming ocean they do not say, "I am this river." In the same way, my son, even though all creatures have come forth from Being, they know not that they have come forth from Being. Whatever a creature may be here, whether tiger or lion or wolf or boar or worm or fly or gnat or mosquito they become that Being again and again. For that Being is the finest essence of all this world and in that Being every creature has its Self. That is reality. That is Ātman. *Tat tvam asi,* Śvetaketu."[68]

There's a lot going on in this story and we might briefly analyze some of its constituents. First, the parable form is used and with that form everything in the story tends to have a double meaning. To begin with, words stand as *signs* for what they point to; thus the word "ocean" is a sign for a body of water into which rivers flow; that is the obvious meaning of "ocean" and "river." But the word "ocean" is also a *symbol* for Being or Brahman, as well, just as "river" is a symbol for Self or Ātman; and that's not obvious at all.

Second, the parable points to a truth with regard to the symbols. That truth is that the rivers are identical with the ocean, i.e., that Self and Ātman and Being and Brahman are identical. Ātman cannot be more fully described because the *Upaniṣads* argue that ultimate Reality, Ātman or Brahman, has no qualities or properties: It transcends all properties since It is the source of every quality and property in the universe. But while the Self cannot be defined and described, It can be experienced and understood.

Third and finally, the Sanskrit phrase *tat tvam asi* means literally "That You are," i.e., Brahman ("tat") and Ātman ("tvam") are identical ("asi"). It is the same conclusion that Uddālaka attempts to drive home to his pupil in each of the five other similar parables that the *Chāndogya* offers. Here is another:

"My son, place this salt in this water and in the morning come to me, once again." Śvetaketu did so. In the morning his father said to him, "That salt that you placed in the water last night, please bring it to me." Śvetaketu looked for it but could not find it, for it was totally dissolved. Then his father said to him, "Please take a sip

> from this end. How does it taste?" "Salty," Śvetaketu replied. "Please take a sip from the middle. How does it taste?" "Salty," he replied again. "Take a sip from that end. How does it taste?" "Salty, as well," he said. Then his father told him to set it aside and then sit with him. Śvetaketu said to him then, "It is everywhere the same." The father replied, "Yes, my son, you do not perceive that Being here but it is truly here, nonetheless. For that invisible essence is the finest essence of all this world, and in that invisible essence every creature has its Self. That is Reality. That is Ātman. Tat tvam asi, Śvetaketu."[69]

There's a lot going on in this parable, as well, but the central point is that Reality, i.e., Brahman, is everywhere, even though It is not perceived by the senses. Discovering or intuitively apprehending Ātman leads to liberation from suffering, and it is that suffering, called *saṁsāra* in the *Upaniṣads,* that drives beings into the search for liberation.

The Indians, like religious people in other traditions, resort to parables and myths to say things and make points that signs and ordinary discourse cannot say or make. The parable, through symbols, directs the listener's attention beyond itself to a truth that must be directly experienced to be understood. It is important, therefore, that one accept the advice of the Chinese sage Lao Tzu when he said, Don't mistake the pointing finger for the moon.

With this brief background behind us, let us turn now to the Rx for liberation from suffering and attempt to order and explain the philosophy and religion that we have seen at work thus far in the *Upaniṣads.*

The Rx for Liberation from Suffering: The Upaniṣads

The Problem

The problem that Upaniṣadic men and women faced was saṁsāra, an ambiguous concept with a profound double meaning. "Saṁsāra" ("a flowing together") means "rebirth" or "transmigration," but since rebirth must go on until mokṣa, liberation, is achieved, it is rebirth that is the chief source of suffering. Hence, saṁsāra comes to mean not only *rebirth* but also the *suffering* that it causes.

Saṁsāra is probably a concept that the Upaniṣadic seers borrowed from the indigenous tribes of the subcontinent. We have suggested earlier that it may be Harappān in origin. All we can really say is that the concept of rebirth is not present in the *Ṛg Veda* and that it was probably unknown to the Āryans. But it appears in the *Upaniṣads* as a well-developed concept.[70]

Here is one of its first appearances in the *Bṛhadāraṇyaka Upaniṣad,* the oldest (ca. 800 B.C.E.) of these "secret teachings." In this *Upaniṣad* we find Śvetaketu, once again, taking instruction with a teacher, a kṣatriya (not a brahmin!, another sign of the religious reformation) named Jaivali, who puts the following curious questions to his śiṣya:

> "Do you know how people here, on dying, separate in different directions?"
> "No," he answered.
> "Do you know how they return to this world?"
> "No," he answered.
> "Do you know why that other world [heaven] is not filled up with the many who go there, again and again?"
> "No," he answered.[71]

And why doesn't heaven fill up with the souls of the dead? A horrendous problem looms that might very well have faced even the Vedic theologians, viz, overcrowding in heaven. The solution that Jaivali and the *Upaniṣads* provide to this portentous catastrophe is, of course, saṁsāra: Selves are constantly being reborn into this sorrowing and sorrowful world, so heaven never fills up. And why are they reborn into this suffering world, again and again? The answer that Jaivali and the *Upaniṣads* provide to this momentous question is the *law of karma:* Selves are constantly getting the justice that they deserve, so they are reborn again and again. This law of cosmic justice is traceable as we mentioned previously, to the Vedic concept of Ṛta.[72] Here is another statement of the law of karma from the *Bṛhadāraṇyaka:*

> Truly, one becomes good by good action, bad by bad action.[73]

But an even more complete statement of what was to become one of the most famous doctrines of later Hinduism was left to a later *Upaniṣad,* the *Śvetāśvatara* (ca. 450 B.C.E.):

> According to its actions, the embodied self *chooses* repeatedly various forms in various conditions in the next life.
>
> According to its own qualities and acts, the embodied self *chooses* the kinds of forms, large and small, that it will take on.[74]

The passage from the *Śvetāśvatara* contains a reference not only to saṁsāra and the law of karma but also to one of the causes of the rebirth, as well: Desire.

The Causes

Kāma

The causes of rebirth and bondage are probably twofold. First, the self is reborn because it chooses to be reborn, that is, it is what one wants or desires; hence desire (kāma) is a major cause of saṁsāra. The *Muṇḍaka Upaniṣad* puts this cause of saṁsāra in this way:

> He who desires desirable things and broods upon them is born again because of that desire.[75]

The *Muṇḍaka* indicates that one will continue to be reborn, dragged back into this suffering world, again and again, until desire for this world ceases.

Avidyā

But desire is not the only cause of bondage. A second cause is ignorance (avidyā). Once again, in the *Muṇḍaka Upaniṣad* the matter of ignorance and knowledge is considered, and considered in such a way as to draw attention to the basic difference between what we have called "brahminism," the Rx for liberation from suffering of the *Vedas,* and what we might now refer to as "Brahmanism," the Rx for liberation from suffering of the *Upaniṣads.* Speaking about the ritual sacrifice, the *Muṇḍaka* declares that when the sacrifice is appropriately carried out, the sacrificer or patron will get what he wants, namely, heaven:

> If one performs the sacrifice in the shining flames and at the right time, these flames will lead him to that place where the single Lord of the Gods presides over all.
>
> Saying "Come, Come," along with pleasing words saying, "This is the heavenly world that you gained by your meritorious works," these carry the sacrificer along the sun's rays [to heaven].

But then comes a warning:

> But those who follow the sacrifice as a way to the highest goal are fools for they fail to understand that the sacrifice rests on inferior karma and they will go to old age and death all over again.

The way of the sacrifice, brahminism, leads back into this world, that is, it leads to saṁsāra. The cause of this rebirth back into suffering is ignorance:

> Those within the midst of ignorance [avidyā], arrogant, puffed up with false learning, these fools, driven by hard times, go around deluded like the blind led by the blind.
>
> Living continually in their own ignorance they think, "We have achieved the greatest of aims!" Because of passion and attachment to the results of karma they do not understand that when their time in heaven is exhausted they are doomed to sink down, once again.

In other words, heaven is no longer the highest goal and the sacrifice is no longer the way to the highest goal:

> Believing falsely that the rites and sacrifices of the *Vedas* are the highest these fools do not understand that other way [knowledge of the Self], so having enjoyed the temporary fruits of heaven they re-enter this world or a lower one.[76]

The *Muṇḍaka*'s stress on knowledge or understanding as the way out of samsara leads to the following singularly important insight: Of the two causes of bondage, ignorance and desire, it is ignorance, the absence of higher knowledge, that is the chief cause of bondage.

Consequently, the person who has conquered ignorance, it would appear, is in a condition superior to the person who has merely conquered desire. If, for example, I conquer desire, I might still be a long way from knowing my true Self. But if I have conquered by knowledge of the Self, then desire is conquered, as well. Hence, the knowledge of the Self would seem to be fundamental to the elimination of desire. We might tentatively conclude, therefore, that in the *Upaniṣads* the fundamental cause of bondage and samsara is ignorance rather than desire.

Māyā

One of the consequences of the existence of avidya is *māyā*. Māyā (the word is cognate with the English words "measure" and "magic") originally meant the magical power with which Brahman both *reveals* and *conceals* Itself in the creation. The *Upaniṣads* argue that Brahman as a Creator projects Itself as the world, thereby revealing Itself in the creation. But at the same time Brahman remains hidden behind that creation such that anyone who mistakes the projection, the creation, for Reality, for Brahman, is suffering from ignorance. The creation is said to be appearance or māyā even though it is produced by the power or māyā of Brahman. To be caught in māyā is to be ensnared in the delusion that the created worlds are Real; it is to mistake this world or heaven for the highest or the ultimately valuable; and it is to be trapped in the shadows of mere appearance.

Consider this story that illustrates by analogy the power of māyā. An anthropologist from Harvard University armed with an assistant, expensive equipment, and a grant from the Ford Foundation, so the story goes, went to India to record on film and on audio tape one of the famous village magicians of south India. These itinerant practitioners of illusion and artful deception (the magicians, not the professors) are as famous in India as are the Houdinis and the Blackstones in the West. The professor, after much trial and error, finally succeeded in locating one such magician and caught up with him in a village in the south during a festival. The professor asked the magician if he would permit him to record the event for which this illusionist was justifiably famous: The Indian rope trick. The magician, for a fee, consented.

The professor set up his equipment near a raised grassy platform that functioned as the magician's stage outside the village. The camera, sound recorder, microphones, tables, tripods, and battery packs which he and his assistant had brought from Cambridge by way of Madras were all in place when the ceremony began. There was hymning and chanting, all recorded, followed by the magician telling the assembled crowd precisely and in detail what he was going to do. The professor understood the language and waited expectantly with the villagers for the performance. And here is what he saw.

The magician, a powerfully built man in his late fifties, climbed to the grassy mound with his grandson, a youth of about twelve. The boy carried a basket which he placed on the ground. The older man took a coiled rope from the basket, unwound it, and threw it up into the air where it stood upright and straight, completely unsupported. The youth then came to the center of the mud-stage and grasping the dangling rope proceeded to climb it. As he reached the top, some fifteen feet above the stage, a white cloud appeared as if out of nowhere and the lad disappeared into it. His grandfather then reached into the basket, drew out a long, heavy, curved knife, put it between his teeth and, in pursuit of the lad, climbed up the rope and disappeared into the white cloud at the top. Immediately the sound of hacking and cutting could be heard. One by one the bloodied limbs, head, and torso of the boy came tumbling out of the cloud and struck the earth. The magician descended, put the knife back into the basket, pulled down the rope, coiled it, and replaced it in the basket as well. He then arranged the bloodied parts of the youth on the ground, clapped his hands three times, the youth leaped to his feet, the crowd applauded and cheered, and the magician passed the hat.

The Harvard professor gathered up his expensive equipment in a state of high excitement. He thanked and paid the magician and returned to Madras where the film was processed. The first and subsequent screenings caused great agitation. For here is what he, and those who saw it, observed. The grandfather appeared on the stage with his grandson who carried the basket. From the basket the magician produced a coiled rope. He made a motion with his arm as if to throw the rope into the air. He laid the rope on the ground. The youth came to the center stage and made some hand-over-hand climbing motions, and then sat down. The older man took the knife from the basket, put it between his teeth and made some climbing motions, as well. Then he made several swinging and chopping motions with the knife, and then he made some climbing down motions, hand-over-hand. He put the knife back into the basket. The boy laid down, the grandfather made some passes over his recumbent body, clapped his hands, the boy leaped up, and they closed the performance to the enthusiastic cheers of the crowd.[77]

How did the magician do it? How did he get a Harvard professor so excited? The answer is that by his māyā he projected what the people expected to see. By his magical power he provided the occasion for the crowd to see what, in its ignorance, it desired. From this point of view it was the spectators themselves who caused the illusion. The magician by his māyā merely provided the occasion, one of the necessary conditions, for the illusion. But from their ignorance of the real situation the spectators caused their own māyā, their own magical deluding illusion: Their ignorance caused them to believe that the spectacle they saw was real; it caused them to feel excitement, loathing, desire, and attachment; it caused them to suffer and feel pain as their fuddled judgment misinterpreted what their senses told them. That's what illusion is: A sensory mis-taking, mis-perceiving. From ignorance, then, pain, pleasure, and suffering resulted as the magician provided the web for appearance and illusion. Saṁsāra, similarly, is a function of ignorance. When one abolishes ignorance by knowledge then saṁsāra disappears.

The Solution

The solution to the problem of saṁsāra, the problem of rebirth and suffering, lies in reaching mokṣa or liberation. In Hinduism, mokṣa is one of the four *arthas* ("aims or goals") of the life of man. These arthas all have a legitimate place within the context of the *āśramas* ("stages") of Hindu life. Before we proceed to discuss mokṣa let us look at these arthas and their place in the āśramas.

The Āśramas

According to a tradition that probably came into existence during the Upaniṣadic period, a human lifetime was ideally meant to span a period of one hundred years; and that century-long life was lived best when it was divided into four periods or stages, the four āśramas, of approximately twenty-five years each. Very briefly, these āśramas are as follows:

Brahmacarya, the student stage. The student of sacred knowledge, like Śvetaketu above, studies with, and may even live with, his guru during the period of study. According to the ancient *Laws of Manu,* from which the doctrine of the āśramas and the arthas receive their fullest expression, the student must obey the following precepts:

- The [student] who has been initiated must be instructed in the performance of the religious vows, and gradually learn the *Veda,* observing the prescribed rules.

- Everyday, having bathed and been purified, he must offer water to the gods, sages and manes [ancestors], worship the gods, and place fuel on the fire.

- Let him abstain from honey, meat, perfumes, garlands of flowers, condiments for flavoring foods, women. . . .[78]

And so on, as the rules for being a student continue.

Gṛhastha, the householder stage. The householder takes wife and children and, since he supports the other three āśramas, lives out the prescribed period of his life working at the vocation inherited from his father. That is to say, if his father is a brahmin (priest or teacher) or a kṣatriya (soldier, prince, or politician) or a vaiśya (merchant or farmer) then so is he, and he practices that vocation during this second āśrama. It is interesting to note that the āśramas, or the *āśramadharma*, the practice of the stages of life, were open only to the so-called *dvija* or twice-born, members of the first three varṇas, but not to the fourth varṇa, the śūdras, or serving class. The āśramas were also open to qualified women but they were closed to the casteless and outcastes.

Vānaprastha, the retirement, or forest dweller, stage. The retired householder spends this stage in a place of retirement. In the Upaniṣadic period it was the forest; in the modern world it would be a retirement retreat where he might follow *Manu*'s prescriptions:

- Abandoning all food raised by cultivation, and abandoning all his belongings, he may depart into the forest, either committing his wife to his sons, or accompanied by her.

- Taking with him the sacred fire and the implements required for domestic sacrifices, he may go forth from the village into the forest and reside there, controlling his senses. . . . In order to attain complete [union with] the Self, [let him study] the various sacred texts contained in the Upaniṣads. . . .[79]

The goal or artha at this āśrama is mokṣa as it is for the fourth and last stage as well.

Sannyāsa, the ascetic wanderer stage. The wandering holy man moves from village to village with his begging bowl, intent only on pursuing mokṣa:

- Having studied the *Vedas* in accordance with the rule [brahmacarya āśrama], having begat sons according to the sacred law [gṛhastha àśrama], and having offered sacrifices according to his ability [vānaprastha āśrama], he may direct his mind to final liberation.

- Departing from his house fully provided with the means of purification, let him wander about absolutely silent, and caring nothing for enjoyments that may be offered [to him.]

- Let him always wander alone, without any companion in order to attain [final liberation], fully understanding that the solitary man, who neither forsakes nor is forsaken, gains his end.

- He shall neither possess a fire, nor a dwelling; he may go to a village for his food, indifferent to everything, firm of purpose, meditating and concentrating his mind on Brahman.[80]

The Arthas

Each of the āśramas has a legitimate (i.e., necessary and acceptable) goal, or artha, at which it aims. These arthas are:

Artha also means "wealth," hence artha is the goal of wealth: property, cattle, gold, sons, and all those material possessions that make the householder life possible and, in turn, that make the other asramas possible as well. Little wonder that Manu, the reputed author of the laws and a mythic synthesis of Noah (Manu survived a gigantic flood) and Moses (he promulgated the law to all mankind who would come after him), says that the householder stage is the most honored. Artha, wealth, is a legitimate goal for all of those in the householder asrama.

Kāma is the goal of sensual love, i.e., sexual desire, for by pursuing kāma the householder produces sons and daughters. Thus contrary to many Western misconceptions about Hinduism, both material goods and sexual enjoyment are honorable and accepted goals within Hinduism, at least for the householder.

Dharma is the goal of duty, i.e., the duty to follow one's vocation and to obey the laws of God and man. It constitutes a legitimate goal for the student, the householder, and the forest dweller, all of whom need the guidance and council of the law. For the ascetic wanderer, the sannyāsi, whose funeral rites have already been celebrated as a sign of his total abandonment of all laws and desires, the goal of dharma has already been transcended.

Mokṣa is the goal of liberation; it constitutes release or freedom from saṁsāra. While liberation is the ultimate aim of all Hindus, it is the immediate goal of the forest hermit and the abandoner. Achieving this goal brings the searcher wisdom and contentment as both ignorance and desire are destroyed and the Self is absorbed into Brahman.

These then are the āśramas and the arthas of Hinduism. The principle texts for the pursuit of the artha of mokṣa, wherein lay the solution to the problem of suffering, were, of course, the *Upaniṣads*. And mokṣa, as far as the central thrust of the *Upaniṣads* is concerned, meant final absorption of the Self into Brahman. Therefore, the solution to the problem of saṁsāra entailed the Real returning to the Real, and mokṣa as absorption was accomplished without the survival of any individual personality, that is, without any personal memory or consciousness. The ultimate goal, as far as the central thrust of the *Upaniṣads* is concerned, is not heaven, then, but blissful oneness with higher Brahman.[81]

The Place of Women in the Hindu Tradition

As might be expected, the *Laws of Manu*, as a guide to Hindu manners, morals, and customs, have something to say about women and their role in society. But what the *Manu* says about women is strangely ambivalent. Beginning with some modestly liberal sentiments *Manu* states:

> Where women are honored, there the Gods are pleased; but where they are not honored, no sacred rite yields any rewards.
>
> Where the female relations live in grief, the family soon completely perishes; but that family where they are not unhappy always prospers.[82]

And this sentiment even continues with some mention of the reason for being good to, but wary of, woman:

> The house on which female relations, not being duly honored, pronounce a curse, perishes completely, as if destroyed by magic.
>
> Hence men who seek [their own] welfare, should always honor women on holidays and festivals with [gifts of] ornaments, clothes, and [dainty] food.[83]

But suddenly, strange misogynous fears and suspicions come creeping out bringing the liberal sentiments to an end:

> Day and night women must be kept in dependence by the males [of] their [families], and, if they attach themselves to sensual enjoyments, they must be kept under one's control.
>
> Her father protects [her] in childhood, her husband protects [her] in youth, and her sons protect [her] in old age: a woman is never fit for independence.[84]

Manu continues, inexplicably placing limits on the freedom and rights of women:

> Him to whom her father may give her, or her brother with her father's permission, she shall obey as long as he lives, and when he is dead, she must not insult his memory.[85]
>
> Though [he be] destitute of virtue, or seeking [his] pleasure [elsewhere] or devoid of good qualities, [yet] a husband must be constantly worshipped as a god by a faithful wife.
>
> . . . if a wife obeys her husband, she will for that [reason alone] be exalted in heaven.[86]

And while a husband may marry again after the death of his wife, the widowed wife is forbidden to do so, and more:

> A faithful wife who desires to dwell with her husband after his death, must never do anything that might displease him who took her hand, whether he be alive or dead.
>
> At her pleasure let her emaciate her body by [living on] pure flowers, roots, and fruit [so that she will not be attractive to other men, apparently]; but she must never even mention the name of another man after her husband has died.[87]

Thus *Manu* on the place of women in the evolving Hindu tradition.

One might ask: Why the ambivalence? What makes *Manu* give with one hand, as if remembering the great female saints, teachers, and renunciates mentioned in the *Upaniṣads,* women with equal opportunity for liberation with men, and then take back with the other? I leave the reader to ponder the ways of ancient man, ways that must sound, unfortunately, strangely modern and familiar.[88]

The Ways

The ways to mokṣa from saṁsāra are found in the practice of two yogas that are often regarded as inseparable. They are dhyāna yoga, the way of meditation, and jñāna yoga, the way of knowledge.

The word "yoga" comes form the Sanskrit root *yuj,* which can mean either "to control," as one might control the ego or the self, or "to join," as one might be absorbed into Brahman in knowing Ātman. The *Upaniṣads* recognize both a lower self (*jīva*) and a higher Self (Ātman, i.e., Brahman). Calming and controlling the self by meditation, dhyāna yoga, enables the Self to be uncovered and known by mystical knowledge, jñāna yoga. The two yogas, in other words, are inseparable for the task of achieving mokṣa, and it is, at times, difficult to separate the two in the Upaniṣadic passages relating to yoga. Dhyāna yoga appears as a kind of propaedeutic, or necessary first stage, for the practice of jñāna yoga: The former leads to calmness and serenity, the latter to mokṣa and enlightenment.

The *Upaniṣads* appear to accept the following model of the self: Imagine the self as a set of four concentric spheres, one inside the other. The innermost sphere is the Ātman, that pure Self, which the meditating yogi is trying to reach. To reach it, however, he must penetrate the three outer layers surrounding that Self. These outer layers are composed of the three *guṇas* ("strands"), the three basic modes or qualities out of which everything is made or woven. Let me say a brief word about these curious entities to which nearly all Indian philosophy, except Buddhism, subscribes.

The Three Guṇas

The guṇas are an odd blending of both physical and moral qualities:

1. *Sattva guṇa* is the strand or quality of goodness, rightness, purity, light, illumination, knowledge, and wisdom, in a word, brightness.

2. *Rajas guṇa* is the strand or quality of "inner lusting, attachment, feelings, jealousy, outer lusting, maliciousness, hatred, . . . envy, insatiability, . . . ambitiousness, . . . and gluttony," in a word, action.

3. *Tamas guṇa* is the strand or quality of "delusion, fear, depression, sleepiness, tiredness, forgetfulness, old age, sorrow, hunger, thirst, anger, heterodoxy [believing false doctrines], ignorance, . . . stupidity . . . ,"[89] in a word, inertia.

Now, every object in the universe, except Brahman-Ātman which is not an object or thing, is composed of all three guṇas; for example, this chair, this book, this table, this light, your self are all composed of all three of the guṇas. In some objects one guṇa predominates, in others another, but they are all three there, nonetheless. For instance, this book that sits unmoving on this table is now actually expressing its tamas guṇa nature. If I move it along the table or drop it from the table, it would exhibit its rajas guṇa nature. And if I set it afire, its glowing brightness would display its sattva guṇa nature. Thus while all three guṇas are present in the book, right now only one is present *actually,* while the remaining two are present *potentially*. If I set the book on fire and then dropped it, two of its guṇas would be present actually, while tamas guṇa, later manifested by inert ashes, would be present but only potentially.

And so it is with all objects including the self. The guṇa picture of the self, as seen in a cross-section under a metaphysical microscope, would look like that set of previously mentioned concentric spheres (see Figure 2.1).

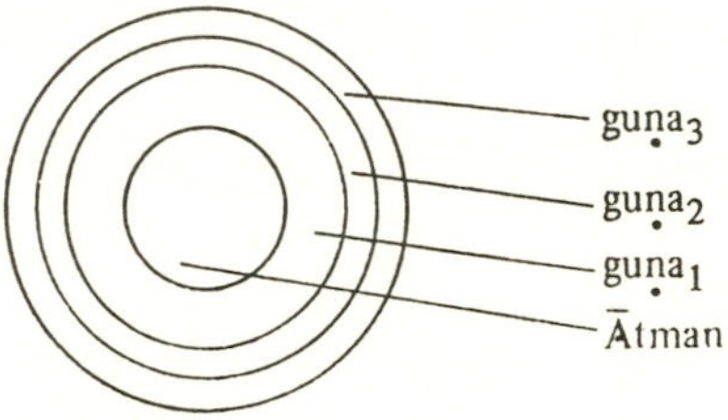

Fig. 2.1 The Self in the *Upaniṣads*

The three guṇas surrounding the Ātman are there in a particular order and in a particular proportion, an order and proportion that would determine precisely whose self it was that was being put under the metaphysical microscope. I would suggest that the three kinds of selves with which we have to deal, the selves of the dvija (twice-born) who are following the āśramas, could be diagramed rather easily following the model presented above. In other words, the brahmin, the teacher-priest, must possess a greater proportion of sattva, the guṇa of knowledge and wisdom, than the other two guṇas, and it would probably be closer to Ātman than the other two guṇas since this proportion and proximity determines both varṇa, or vocation, and self-nature, or personality. The kṣatriya, the warrior-king, prince, or politician, must possess a greater proportion of rajas, the guṇa of energy and action, and it would probably be closer to Ātman than the other two guṇas. And, finally, the vaiśya, the merchant-trader-farmer, must possess a greater proportion of tamas, the guṇa of acquisitiveness and skill-in-generating-wealth, and it would probably be closer to Ātman than the other two guṇas.

The Yogas

But now to the yogas. Their aim is to penetrate the guṇa layers composing the self, and to pierce to the very heart of the self, that is, to the Self or Ātman. Here is the *Muṇḍaka Upaniṣad,* once again:

> Take up the great weapon, the *Upaniṣads,* as the bow, fix on it the arrow sharpened by meditation. Draw it back with a thought directed to the very center of Reality and then penetrate to that Unchanging Target.
>
> The mystic "Om" is the bow, the arrow is the self, Brahman-Ātman is the target. By the undistracted and disciplined person the Target is to be penetrated and the shooter become at-one with it as the arrow [in the Target].[90]

The *Śvetāśvatara Upaniṣad* uses a beautiful and expressive metaphor to indicate what it is that occurs in the act of meditating through the guṇa layers to the heart of Being within. The self is likened to a piece of wood on which the fire-drill (a device for generating fire, familiar to boy and girl scouts the world over) of Om is to act, thereby producing heat, light, fire, illumination, and brightness.

> Just as the potential fire lies hidden in the wood, it is not seen, but it may be brought forth and seized, again and again, by means of the fire drill used on that wood, so also does the Self have to be seized in the body by the use of the mantram "Om."

And how is this to be done?

> By making your body the wood and the mantram "Om" the fire drill, by practicing the art of meditation in this way you will come to see the bright and fiery God hidden deep in yourself.[91]

Finally, there is this passage from the *Maitrī Upaniṣad* (ca. 450 B.C.E.), which lists a series of stages to be passed through for the yogi who would practice meditation, and it states the goal for the sake of which these stages are followed:

> The way to the uniting of the Ātman and the Brahman is this: The control of the breath [*prāṇāyāma*]; the withdrawal of the activity of the senses [*pratyāhāra*]; meditation [*dhyāna*]; concentration [*dhāraṇā*]; contemplation [*tarka*]; and finally absorption [*samādhi*] into that ultimate unity of Brahman and Ātman. This is the sixfold way of yoga.[92]

But samādhi is not the only result of meditational yoga effectively practiced. The *Upaniṣads* catalogue at some length the happy consequences of meditation that range from the ability to produce an inner heat enabling the yogi to stay constantly warm whatever the outside temperature, to success in any undertaking or venture, to eternal bliss and happiness, to mystical union with Brahman. The *Maitrī* states, again:

> By the practice of yoga one attains to contentment, the ability to withstand the pulls and strains of the world's opposites [love-hate, good-evil, hot-cold, success-failure, pleasure-pain, etc.], and supreme tranquility.[93]

The *Upaniṣads* seem then to set forth rather clearly two things with respect to the ways or yogas to the solution of the problem of suffering. First, jñāna yoga leads to knowledge of the identity of the Ātman in one's self with Brahman, and this, in turn, leads to absorption into Brahman and liberation from saṁsāra. The liberation thus achieved is permanent and unalterable. One becomes a jīvanmukta, a liberated-while-yet-alive being.

Second, dhyāna yoga leads to temporary absorption (samādhi) into Brahman, producing states of tranquility, but it does not, in itself, produce mokṣa; rather it gives only a taste or glimpse of mokṣa. The states achieved by meditation, such as samādhi, as opposed to states achieved by mystical intuition or jñāna, last only as long as one is in samadhi. But dhyāna is, nonetheless, a stage on the road to final and ultimate knowledge of the identity between Self and Brahman.[94]

If we now combine what we have learned about the guṇa natures, as determined by the guṇas, and the varṇas, as determined by one's previous life and the law of karma, and the two yogas of knowledge and meditation, then we discover that the *Upaniṣads* appear to be saying that since the chief cause of saṁsāra is ignorance, then it would follow that those guṇa natures with a preponderance of sattva guṇa, the quality of wisdom and knowledge (the brahmins) have a much greater chance for mokṣa than those with a preponderance of rajas guṇa (the kṣatriyas) and tamas guṇa (the vaiśyas).

Table 2.3 **Guṇas and Yogas in the *Upaniṣads***

Predominant Guṇa	Representative Varṇa	Appropriate Yoga	Expected Result	Escape from Saṁsāra?
Sattva	brahmin	jñāna	mokṣa	yes
Rajas	kṣatriya,	dhyāna	mokṣa?/samādhi	?/no
Tamas	vaiśya	dhyāna	mokṣa?/samādhi	?/no
Tamas	śūdra, non-dvijas	?	?	no

Consider Table 2.3 which attempts to summarize the relation between the guṇas, varṇas, yogas, expected results, and the chances of escape from saṁsāra. Reading across the table from left to right, it is clear that brahmins with a predominance of sattva guṇa have a greater chance to dispel ignorance through jñāna yoga and thereby escape saṁsāra than either the kṣatriya or the vaiśya. The *Upaniṣads* do not appear to rule out mokṣa for the remaining dvija but their guṇa natures, on the whole, do not seem to fit them for escaping ignorance and desire by the same yoga used by the brahmins.

Further, these two latter dvijas are fitted by their guṇa natures for the experience of Brahman, a glimpse of Brahman, in samādhi; but such glimpses do not allow them to escape saṁsāra.

Finally, the *Upaniṣads* do not provide a way of liberation for the non-dvija, that is, for the low class sudras or for the outcaste untouchables and *caṇḍālas* (corpse carriers) or for the noncaste non-Hindus and non-Indians.

In conclusion, the *Upaniṣads* seem to be as exclusive for brahmins, kṣatriyas, and vaiśyas as the *Vedas* seem to have been previously for the brahmins. The way would appear to be open for a religious reformation, once again, and that reformation comes with the *Bhagavad Gītā*, which manages to find more definite appropriate yogas, expected results, and escapes from saṁsāra for, not only kṣatriyas and vaiśyas, but for non-dvijas, non-Hindus, and non-Indians alike.

The Guiding Principle: The Law of Karma

The principle that appears to guarantee that following the yogas will lead to mokṣa is the law of karma. It is important to remember that the law of karma does guarantee that since actions produce consequences, no effort, however small it may be, is in vain. Thus right efforts rightly applied yield right results; and appropriate yogas rightly applied lead to their expected results.

Before leaving the *Upaniṣads* a summary of the results of our inquiry thus far can be found in Table 2.4.

Table 2.4 **The Rx for Liberation from Suffering: The *Upaniṣads***

Problem:	Saṁsāra as suffering in this world and rebirth in the next
Causes:	Ignorance (avidyā) of Self is the chief cause of saṁsāra with desire (kāma), i.e., lusting for anything that is not Self, as a secondary cause.
Solution:	Mokṣa, liberation, as mystical absorption into Brahman and release from saṁsāra
Ways:	Jñāna yoga, the way of knowledge of the identity of the real Self with Brahman, and also dhyāna yoga, the way of meditation, which leads to glimpses of mokṣa, i.e., samādhi
Guiding Principle or Person:	The law of karma

Summary

As the Upaniṣadic religion (Brahmanism) evolved out of Vedism (brahminism), it seems to have fallen into the same trap of exclusivity that may have called it into existence to begin with. While suffering may be temporally assuaged through meditation and samādhi, the results produced are not permanent. That permanent condition seems to be possible only for those whose guṇa nature is fitted for the yoga of knowledge that leads to mokṣa. Brahmanism has identified the causes of saṁsāra as ignorance and desire with the apparent stress on the former; but since ignorance can only be conquered by knowledge, and since that ability depends on one's guṇa nature, the way to knowledge and the release from saṁsāra would appear to be the exclusive prerogative, once again, of the brahmins.

In the important business of discovering who we are, that we are Tigers not sheep, that our innermost nature is divine and not devilish or mundane, the Hindus will have to discover another method for revealing that nature with a new set of yogas to be added to those already available. It will remain for the *Bhagavad Gītā* to make that discovery and reveal those yogas. It will also be the *Gītā*'s task to synthesize the three traditions that we have been describing throughout this book. Those traditions are the Indus and the pre-Vedic tradition that leads to bhakti, or devotional, yoga, and to Swami Bhaktivedanta; the brahmin or Vedic tradition that leads to karma, or unselfish action, yoga, and to Mohandas Gandhi; and, finally, the Brahman or Upaniṣadic tradition that leads to jñāna, or mystical knowledge, yoga, and to Ramana Maharshi.

3

The Synthesis of Bhaktism, Brahminism, and Brahmanism: The *Bhagavad Gītā* (ca. 200 B.C.E.)

The *Bhagavad Gītā* (from *bhagavan*, "God," *gītā*, "song" or "chant," hence "the song of God") is drawn from a brief part of India's greatest, and the world's longest, epic poem, the *Mahābhārata*, a work composed by the master poet Vyāsa. This vast and sprawling epic constitutes the history of the ancient Indian people, serving somewhat the same function as the *Old Testament*, so called, for Jews or the *Iliad* and the *Odyssey* for Greeks. It contains the myths, legends, folk lore, and the religious and philosophic history of India. In over 100,000 metrical verses the *Mahābhārata* focuses on two blood-related families and the powerful and deadly interactions between the members of those two families. The climax of this work is a terrible war involving tens of thousands of warriors, a holocaust from which there will be only a few survivors. The war pits the family of the Pāṇḍavas, the good guys, against the family of the Kauravas, the bad guys. The story of their interaction goes something like this: The Pāṇḍava family had lost their kingdom to the Kauravas after being cheated by a Kauvara uncle. Because of their loss, they are compelled to wander for thirteen years throughout India with the promise that their lands will be returned to them after that time. The adventures that occur during their wanderings, grotesque as well as romantic adventures, form a major portion of the epic itself. The five Pāṇḍava brothers, the heroes of the epic, return after the period of exile is over but their Kaurava relatives refuse to abide by the original agreement. After all attempts at a compromise fail, the two families go to war.

The Story

The *Bhagavad Gītā* is drawn from Chapters 23 to 40 of the section called *Bhīṣma parvan* of the *Mahābhārata*. As the *Gītā* opens, we find the two armies, 100,000 men on the Kaurava side and 70,000 on the Pāṇḍava side, drawn up, facing each other, ready for the battle that will decide the right and, in the process, destroy almost all of them. The events that occur are related to the blind Kaurava king by his chief minister, and what the minister recounts is the dialogue that takes place between two of the warriors.

So far there does not seem to be anything about the *Gītā* that would make it the most popular religious text in India and one of the greatest devotional works the world has ever known. But wait. One of the warriors is the human hero of the *Bhagavad Gītā,* one of the five Pāṇḍava brothers named Arjuna. And his companion, his charioteer and kinsman, is in reality a God named Kṛṣṇa. Arjuna is not aware of the divine nature of Kṛṣṇa at the outset of the poem but this is gradually revealed to him as the action progresses throughout the eighteen chapters and 700 verses of the *Bhagavad Gītā.*

The dramatic and philosophical tension is initiated when Arjuna, at the end of the first chapter of the *Gītā,* filled with despondency and fear, sinks down on the floor of his chariot and refuses to take part in the battle. The remaining seventeen chapters recount Kṛṣṇa's attempts to persuade Arjuna to do his duty as a warrior and to defend the rights of the Pāṇḍava clan against the Kauravas.

In the conclusion to the *Mahābhārata* Arjuna does finally fight in the battle, which lasts eighteen days. He kills one of the chief Kaurava leaders, a cousin, and the Pāṇḍavas win. Funerals and lamentations follow and the work ends as the leader of the Pāṇḍavas, Arjuna's brother, is crowned king.

But why, initially, does Arjuna refuse to fight? And how and why does Kṛṣṇa persuade him to fight? Who are these two heroes, one human and one divine? And why has this work been called "the greatest religious work in the history of the world?" These are some of the questions with which we shall be dealing as we examine the philosophy and religion of the *Bhagavad Gītā.*

The *Gītā,* as we have indicated above, is an attempt to blend three previous, and apparently unblendable, traditions--bhaktism, brahminism, and Brahmanism. I say unblendable for these three previous traditions seem patently inconsistent with one another in the sense that if one tradition *alone* is true or right, then the other two traditions must be wrong. For example, if the Gods *alone* are real and if man's highest happiness is reached through action *alone* then the other two traditions must be wrong when they say either that one personal God *alone* is ultimately real or that impersonal Brahman *alone* is ultimately real and that God and Brahman are reached by either devotion or knowledge, respectively. So how, on this interpretation, does one blend the unblendable?

In order to get started here, let us compare the results thus far with respect to the Rx for the liberation from suffering for bhaktism, brahminism, and Brahmanism. I indicate in Table 3.1 in summary fashion what we have found in our three previous traditions. The differences are manifold and any blending or synthesizing that is going to occur would have to be rather ingenious, it would seem. But the *Gītā* is, if nothing else, ingenious.

Table 3.1 **The Rx for Liberation from Suffering: Bhaktism, brahminism, Brahmanism**

	Bhaktism	brahminism	Brahmanism
Problem:	Suffering as concern about life after death and anxiety over survival in this life	Anxiety about getting wealth in this world and heaven in the next	Saṁsāra as suffering in this world and rebirth in the next
Cause:	Realizing that certain powers and forces are threatening and uncontrollable	Disobedience to the laws of God and man and neglect of the ritual sacrifice	Avidyā as the chief cause and kāma as the secondary cause
Solution:	Achieving a better future life and gaining power over those threatening forces	Gaining power in this world and the next	Mokṣa as absorption into Brahman and release from saṁsāra

Ways:	Propitiation of the Gods and forces of nature through bhakti yoga	Leading a moral life and paying attention to the Gods through action, i.e., prayer and sacrifice	Dhyāna yoga and jñāna yoga
Guiding Principle or Person:	Unknown, though possibly a personal God or power in nature	Ṛta and Lord Varuṇa, among others	The law of karma

Dilemmas and Arguments

Let me set out the simple details of Arjuna's refusal to fight and Kṛṣṇa's attempts to persuade him to fight. As the arguments flow back and forth, it becomes clear that the author of the *Gītā* is trying to portray his two heroes as something more than mere individuals. They emerge as types, as symbolic representations. Kṛṣṇa is God, the voice of the Divine, speaking to mankind, calling to humans everywhere, drawing all who have ears to hear His message. And Arjuna, of course, is man, the voice of any man or woman who has ever been caught in a moral or personal problem wherein no matter which way they run, they cannot escape their problem. So, what is Arjuna's problem?

Arjuna has his charioteer drive their chariot between the two armies shortly before the battle is to begin. Assured of victory, he wants to see the enemy that he will soon defeat; and what he sees horrifies him, overwhelms his confidence, stifles his courage. For facing him across the battleline are people that he knows and loves; friends and teachers, uncles and cousins. The war is, one is reminded, a civil war wherein everyone, heroes and villains, attackers and defenders, is related to everyone else.

> Thus seeing these kinsmen standing there, ready to fight each other,
> Arjuna
>
> Was moved to pity and love for those he saw. Utterly despondent he spoke and said: Seeing my family, my brothers all, Oh Kṛṣṇa, drawn up here, eager to kill one another,

> My arms drop down, my mouth becomes dry, my whole body trembles and my hair rises in horror.
>
> My bow, Gāndīva, slips from my hands and my flesh is on fire. I am unable to stand and my mind is reeling.
>
> I have forebodings of evil, Oh Kṛṣṇa, for I see no good whatsoever in slaying my family in battle.[95]

Arjuna then gives his reason for refusing to fight and it has to do with the consequences of the destruction of the family: For if the family is destroyed, as it surely will be, then the dharma or traditional laws of the family will perish and lawlessness will prevail; if lawlessness prevails, then the women of the family will be corrupted, and with that corruption there arises a confusion of the varṇas as the women give birth to children without knowing who their fathers are. With this bastardly mixing of the varṇas two things will happen: First, the souls of the living will go to hell as punishment for their corruption of the women and the varṇas; and second, the souls of the dead ancestors will also fall into hell, deprived, as they will surely be, of the sacrifices of the rice and water that support and maintain those souls. Arjuna concludes:

> Thus by these deeds of the destroyer of the family, deeds which produce a confusion of the varṇas, the laws of varṇa are broken, and with that the eternal family laws are abolished.
>
> When these ancient family customs are abolished then all men are doomed to live in hell. . . .
>
> Ah, see what a great sin we are about to commit, to kill our brothers in order to greedily enjoy the kingship.
>
> Far better it would be for me if, unarmed and unresisting, [the Kaurava's] sons, with their weapons in their hands, should slay me in the battle.

The first chapter of the *Bhagavad Gītā* then concludes:

> Having said this, Arjuna, in the midst of the battlefield, sat down on the floor of his chariot, casting aside his bow and arrows, his heart overcome with grief.[96]

So far, in our pursuit of Arjuna's problem, all we have is a moral dilemma; and, at this point, it is difficult to see how one of the world's greatest spiritual poems could possibly be built out of the attempt to get an ancient warrior off his haunches and back into a long-forgotten, and possibly mythical, battle.

But the point, again, is that it is at the symbolic level that events must be understood here. If we take the text too literally, much of its significance, charm, and penetrating message will be lost. Arjuna and Kṛṣṇa are not only types standing symbolically for man and God, respectively, but the battlefield itself must be seen in the same metaphorical sense. The battlefield is within the heart of every person; and the problem that Arjuna faces symbolizes the problems that we all face, beginning, perhaps, with the problem of just getting out of bed in the morning in order to hack away at the day's other problems. The *Gītā*'s message, Lord Kṛṣṇa's message, to every human being is that there are good reasons to hack, and that happiness and salvation, meaning and moksa, can be found through that very hacking.

Arjuna faces three dilemmas, namely, a family dilemma, a personal dilemma, and a dilemma of action. Let us consider each of them.

The Family Dilemma

The family dilemma is: No matter what Arjuna does on the battlefield, the family of Pāṇḍavas and Kauravas is doomed. The family dilemma looks like this.

1. If Arjuna fights then the family is destroyed.
2. If Arjuna doesn't fight then the family is also destroyed.
3. Arjuna must either fight or not fight.
4. Therefore, either way, the family is destroyed.

I would suggest that the family dilemma, the dilemma that initially motivates the entire dialogue between Arjuna and his divine charioteer, receives short shrift from Kṛṣṇa for he dismisses the entire concern that Arjuna has for his family, the good guys as well as the bad guys. The dismissal occurs when Kṛṣṇa says, in effect: Don't worry about the family; the wise man does not worry about either the living or the dead. We shall return to this dismissal shortly. Attention is then focused on the second dilemma, the personal dilemma.

The Personal Dilemma

The personal dilemma is: No matter what Arjuna does on the battlefield, he is doomed. The personal dilemma looks like this.

1. If Arjuna fights then he will be fighting his family, and then he's doomed.

2. If Arjuna does not fight then he will have failed to protect his family, and then he's doomed.

3. Arjuna must either fight or not fight.

4. Therefore, he's doomed.

The point is that the very family that Arjuna is called upon as a ksatriya to serve and protect is the very family that Arjuna is called upon to kill and obliterate. And it is this personal dilemma that Kṛṣṇa attacks as he offers arguments for meeting that dilemma in Chapter II of the *Gītā*. Before we turn to the third dilemma, the dilemma of action, let us see how Kṛṣṇa attempts to solve the first two dilemmas that Arjuna now faces.

Two Brahmanical Arguments

Kṛṣṇa offers two arguments to meet Arjuna's despondency and the dilemma that he faces. Kṛṣṇa begins by attacking both the family dilemma and the personal dilemma with what we might call "the live forever argument:"

> You are mourning for those that are not to be mourned for, and you speak wise words in vain. The truly wise mourn for neither the living nor the dead.
>
> For there never was a time when I or you or these kings did not exist. And never shall we cease to be, hereafter.[97]

At this point Arjuna may be justifiably bewildered. Just who is the "I," the "you," and the "we" that are going to live forever? There are two possible choices: First, Kṛṣṇa could be referring to Arjuna's *jīva*, that is, his soul, ego, or personality, that part of him that will survive the death of the body, go on to heaven or hell or the realm of the ancestors, and live there, just as the *Vedas* have described it, with its memories, desires, and consciousness intact. That's one possibility that Kṛṣṇa's argument seems to offer as he says, in effect, Don't worry, Arjuna, whatever happens the family is going to live forever and you are also going to live forever; therefore, fight!

Second, Kṛṣṇa could be referring to Ātman, the impersonal but imperishable Self, that aspect of Brahman, as the *Upaniṣads* described It, that lives within all beings and that can never die. That is another possibility that Kṛṣṇa's statement seems to offer as he says, in effect, Don't worry, Arjuna, whatever happens, the real Self will live forever; therefore, fight! As mentioned previously, the *Gītā* is attempting to weave together both the Vedic and the Upaniṣadic prescriptions for liberation, and here it seems to offer a choice between the two to Arjuna. The following passages expand on this insistent ambiguity in the pronouns of the previous passages as Kṛṣṇa continues:

> Just as the Dweller in this body has passed from childhood to youth to old age, in just the same way shall that One pass on eventually to another body. The wise man is not deceived in this matter.[98]

What or who is the Dweller (dweller) and the One (one)? There are no capital letters in Sanskrit, so the question then is, Are these passages referring to the Self, in which case capital letters would be justified, or do they refer to the self, in which case no honorific initial letters would be employed?

Kṛṣṇa continues with a second argument, an argument against the personal dilemma, that we might call "the metaphysical priorities argument." The metaphysical priorities argument simply draws attention to the importance of the Ātman or the embodied Dweller, *dehin,* as the only real entity in the universe. The argument attempts to get Arjuna to see that in comparison to this Dweller nothing else is either real or important, not family, not ancestors, not his body, and not himself. The metaphysical priorities argument seeks to set Arjuna straight on that which is most needful in his situation:

> That which is truly unreal can never come into being; and that which is truly real can never cease to be. This truth about the unreal and the real has been seen by the truly wise.
>
> Know this, that which lies immanent within all this world, that Reality can never cease to be. No one can bring about the destruction of that imperishable Reality.
>
> These material bodies of the eternal, indestructible and immeasurable embodied Dweller within are themselves unreal. Therefore, fight, Oh Arjuna.[99]

The family dilemma that showed Arjuna's concern for the living and the dead family, and the personal dilemma that stated his concern for himself are both drowned in a flood of metaphysics as the description of this Dweller, or the One, continues:

> He who believes this One a slayer and he who believes It slain, neither of these understand: this One neither slays nor is It slain.
>
> It is not born, nor does It die, nor having been can It ever cease to be. Unborn, unending, eternal, this primordial One is not slain when the body is slain.
>
> And he who knows this One as indestructible and eternal, as unborn and imperishable, how can such a man, Oh Arjuna, slay or cause to be slain?
>
> Just as a man casts aside worn-out clothes to put on new ones, so the Dweller within casts aside worn-out bodies and enters into others that are new.[100]

The family dilemma is put to rest and the personal dilemma is solved by virtue of getting straight on metaphysical priorities, on what is important and what is not. The Dweller within is Real, Kṛṣṇa says, hence it can never be hurt, harmed, or injured; therefore, fight!

> This Dweller in the body of everyone, Oh Arjuna, can never be slain. Therefore you should not mourn for any creatures [including your family and yourself].[101]

But a gnawing question remains after all this Brahmanical metaphysical speculation about the Dweller and Its nature is finished: Did Arjuna really understand what Kṛṣṇa was talking about? Arjuna is an Āryan soldier, wise in warfare and battle tactics; he is not a brahmin, learned in the *Upaniṣads* and their subtle discussions of the Real. When all of the arguments and counter arguments are finished, Arjuna, in frustrated bewilderment, suddenly cries out to his teacher:

> You seem only to confuse my understanding with your perplexing words. So tell me clearly, what is the one way by which I may attain the highest [*śreyas*]?[102]

It appears that the Brahmanical arguments have gone over Arjuna's warrior head.

Four brahminical Arguments

To answer the question that Arjuna has asked, Kṛṣṇa now offers four new arguments against the personal dilemma. These arguments seem brahminical or Vedic in origin and they are undoubtedly brought out because Arjuna missed the Brahmanical or Upaniṣadic point about the imperishable Dweller within and because Kṛṣṇa knows that he will not miss arguments aimed to appeal to his Āryan, martial nature. He is, after all, a plain man, a plainspoken man, a commonsensical, down-to-earth warrior, and what Kṛṣṇa now says is meant to appeal to that plain kṣatriya, rajas guṇa nature in Arjuna.

The first argument is the duty-calls argument:

> Further, looking to your own duty as a warrior you must not falter. For there is nothing better for a kṣatriya than a just war.[103]

The appeal here is to Arjuna's sense of duty. The war would be a just war for Arjuna because duty (dharma) calls him to fulfill his role as a warrior. But the duty-calls argument accomplishes nothing against the family dilemma since duty calls all kṣatriyas to the battlefield and that universal call will lead, as Arjuna has seen, to the destruction of the entire family. Finally, the duty-calls argument accomplishes nothing against the personal dilemma for that dilemma points to Arjuna's own destruction and dooming if he does fulfill his role as a warrior. So much for the duty-calls argument.

The second argument advanced by Kṛṣṇa is the heaven-can-be-yours argument:

> The chance to fight here is an open door to heaven for you. Fortunate, indeed, Oh Arjuna, are those warriors who get such a chance.[104]

The third argument is the sin-will-be-yours argument:

> But now if you will not engage in this just war, if you will not perform your duty and instead abandon that duty and your honor, then you will surely fall into sin.[105]

Finally, the fourth argument, is the shame-will-be-yours argument:

> [If you do not fight] men will tell again and again of your eternal dishonor; and for one now held in high regard, such disgrace is worse than death.
>
> The warriors of the great chariots will think that you fled from the battle through fear. And to those who have held you in high esteem, you will from this time forward be regarded as a coward.
>
> And many things it would be improper to say, your enemies will say of you, slandering your honor. What now could be more terrible than that?[106]

Kṛṣṇa concludes all of these arguments, the duty-calls argument, the heaven-can-be-yours argument, the sin-will-be-yours argument, and the shame-will-be-yours argument by stating what the happy alternative can be:

> If you die fighting, you shall win heaven; and if you live and conquer, you shall win earth. Therefore, arise, Oh Arjuna, resolve to fight.[107]

But all of the latter three arguments fail and they fail for the very reason that the latter first argument, the duty-calls argument, failed: The family that Arjuna is duty-bound to protect, and that is the source of the call to duty, getting into heaven, and escaping sin and shame, is the very same family that Arjuna is called upon to destroy; and that is the source of the failure to do his duty, of not getting into heaven, and of not escaping sin and shame. Neither the family dilemma nor the personal dilemma are solved by any of these arguments. That is the problem and Arjuna is stuck with it, and so, it must seem, is Kṛṣṇa.

With the failure of these four brahminical arguments, and with Arjuna's apparent failure to understand the two Brahmanical arguments, in solving either the family dilemma or the personal dilemma, Kṛṣṇa switches tactics. We turn then to the third dilemma mentioned above.

The Dilemma of Action

The dilemma of action is the generalization of the personal dilemma. It says: No matter what we do, whether we do good or evil, we are doomed.

The dilemma of action looks like this:

1. If one does evil acts (such as destroying members of one's own family) then this produces evil results that entail bondage and rebirth.

2. If one does good acts (such as doing one's duty and protecting members of one's own family) then this produces good results that also entail bondage and rebirth.

3. One must either do evil acts or good acts.

4. Therefore, whatever one does, bondage and rebirth are the results.

The dilemma of action is going to carry us and our two heroes into philosophic and religious areas beyond battlefields, beyond just wars and duty, beyond even heaven, sin, and shame.

Karma Yoga

The problem that Arjuna faces can now be seen in a new and wider perspective as Kṛṣṇa reminds his companion of a point that we saw previously in our discussion of the *Upaniṣads:* The brahminical heaven that is reached through good acts does not solve the Brahmanical problem of saṁsāra. Perhaps recognizing that all of his previous arguments were in vain, Kṛṣṇa suddenly alters the attack from a discussion about pleasure and pain, honor and dishonor, to a discussion about action and the bondage of karma:

> But now hear from me of the knowledge of the method of yoga, joined with which, Oh Arjuna, you shall let loose the bonds of karma.[108]

This yoga of karma by which, as we shall see, both the personal dilemma and the dilemma of action are to be solved is a method of acting that attacks the third premises of both dilemmas. It denies the premises that stated that on the one hand Arjuna must either fight or not fight (the personal dilemma) and on the other that one must either do evil acts or good acts (the dilemma of action). The yoga that denies these premises and slips between the horns of both dilemmas is called "karma yoga."

Karma yoga is a way of acting that does not involve acting in the ordinary sense of that term. It has been called "actionless action," and for good reason. Kṛṣṇa now begins his discussion of karma yoga:

> Those whose souls are filled with desires, intent only on heaven as their goal, their way offers only rebirth as the result of their actions. They offer only various rituals for obtaining their goals of pleasure and power.

> The *Vedas* have the three gunas as their concern. Be free from these three binding qualities, Oh Arjuna. Be free from the pairs of opposites, attached only to the truth, free from gaining and coveting things, attached only to Ātman.
>
> The *Vedas* are as much use to an enlightened brahmin as a tank of water in a place flooded on all sides by water.[109]

Following this unsubtle attack on the *Vedas,* and having stated that desire and the gunas are what cause bondage and that heaven is only a temporary haven in the milieu of saṁsāra, Kṛṣṇa launches into a description of the yoga that will lead Arjuna, and all human beings for that matter, to liberation:

> Let your concern be with action alone and never with the fruits of action. Do not let the results of action be your motive, and do not be attached to inaction.
>
> Firmly fixed in yoga, Oh Arjuna, perform your actions renouncing attachments, indifferent to success and failure. This balanced indifference is called [karma] yoga.
>
> For mere action is inferior by far to the yoga of unattachment, Oh Arjuna. In this attitude of unattachment seek your refuge. Pitiable, indeed, are those whose motive is the fruit of action.
>
> Those endowed with unattachment leave behind in this world both good and evil. Therefore, unite yourself to [karma] yoga. [Karma] yoga is, indeed, skill in action.
>
> The wise, united to unattachment, renounce the fruits which action produces, and freed thereby from the bondage of rebirth, they go to that place free from pain.[110]

What Kṛṣṇa is saying is that by letting go of the desire for the results of one's actions, the karmic results ordinarily generated by the action cease to exist. When karmic results cease to exist, the law of karma becomes inapplicable to the action and, as a result, acts do not lead to bondage and rebirth: The dilemma of action is solved and with it the personal dilemma is solved as well.

The Nature of Action

There are several assumptions buried in this new yoga that can be profitably explored. Let us talk about an *action* as an event consisting of three parts: motive, act, and consequences. The *motive* is the desire that the agent has that starts the act and brings about results. The motive can be morally good or bad or neutral. Suppose I see a very old person waiting to cross a busy street. Suppose that I resolve to help him get to the other side; then my motive is good. Or suppose that I resolve to push him into the traffic; then my motive is bad. Or suppose that I resolve to ignore him; then, conceivably, my motive is neutral, that is, ignoring a person, ordinarily, is not a moral activity.

The *act* is merely the happening or activity of putting the motive into the world. In our example, it would involve taking the older person's arm, making my intentions clear, walking the person across the street and depositing him on the sidewalk safely. Or it could involve pushing the older person into the traffic. Or it could involve ignoring the person entirely. The act could be morally good, bad, or neutral as well.

The criteria for judging both motive and act as morally good, bad, or neutral is rather complicated. Suffice it to say that the criteria depend on the existence of, and our awareness of, a moral rule that specifies that motives or acts of a certain kind are always good or always bad. Thus there may be a rule that says, Thou shalt desire to help older people to cross streets. Or a rule that says, Thou shalt help older people to cross streets. If I intended to help an older person cross the street, or if I helped an older person cross the street, then, conceivably, my motive and act would both be good by virtue of being endorsed by the moral rule. Similarly, failing to abide by the rules for motive and act would produce the contrary result, i.e., bad motives and bad acts.

Or, if there were no such rules regarding moral motives and acts, both could be judged by the consequences which they, in turn, produce. Thus, the *utilitarian* in ethics holds that good consequences and bad consequences will be the only criteria that we need for judging the goodness or badness of an action. If the older person, as a result of my help, is happy on reaching the other side of the street, then the action as a whole was good. Which brings us to the consequences.

The *consequences* are the short-range or long-range results of the motive and the act. Short-range consequences of the act of getting the older person across the street might be the feelings he has on reaching the sidewalk, the heart attack that he might subsequently have on entering a store across the street, the bumping into, and consequent immobilizing of, a hold-up man in the store as he falls from his heart attack, and so on. Consequences of an act can go on into the future for as long as matter and space continue to exist. For our purposes, however, and for the purposes that the *Gītā* has with respect to karma yoga, the only consequences that we need to consider here are the short-range consequences. And of the short-range consequences that we need to consider only those which are actually intended by the agent are important for understanding karma yoga.

In the ordinary workings of things my motive brings about an act that then produces consequences. The entire action is successful for the agent, if the motive is in some sense congruent with the consequences, i.e., the action is successful if the agent gets what he desired, and unsuccessful otherwise. Furthermore, a successful or unsuccessful action can be judged wrong or right depending on whether there are moral rules forbidding or supporting what was desired or produced; or, lacking such moral rules, judgments of moral worth can be based on the happy or unhappy consequences that result. Finally, the moral or immoral consequences of motive and act produce karmic results that must be punished or rewarded. It is important to remember that the *Gītā,* like the *Upaniṣads* previously and the *Vedas* before that, claims that the universe is a just place in which everyone, sooner or later, gets his due. Every human action has consequences, and within the action both motive and act produce consequences that must be paid for or rewarded depending on their moral worth.

Thus if I help the older person to cross the street, I accumulate merit in the form of good karma. And if I were to have the heart attack and die after the completion of this good act, and if justice is to be done in the universe, then I must be rewarded. But if I am dead, then the reward must be done in my next life. If I am not rewarded in my next life, then the universe is not a just place. But it is a just place. Therefore, the reward must be done in my next life; I must be brought back to suffer the reward.

And this carries us back then to the dilemma of action: Whether one does right actions or wrong actions with good or bad motives and acts, one is chained to bondage and rebirth. Golden chains are still chains and, whether one is reborn into the best of all possible worlds as a karmic reward or into the worst of all possible worlds as a karmic punishment, one is still in chains.

But now karma yoga proposes to undercut the entire action situation by showing that it is possible to act without desire for the consequences. The act still produces consequences but in the absence of the agent's motive or desire no karmic residue remains, and, therefore, no bondage occurs, and, therefore, no rebirth is necessary. Rebirth ceases when the karmic bank account is emptied. That is to say, saṁsāra, the problem faced by Arjuna and by all human beings if the *Gītā* is right, ceases when there is no bad karma to be punished and no good karma to be rewarded.

The Jīvanmukta

The goal is the performance of karmaless or karma-neutral acts, i.e., spontaneous acts as natural and free as automatic acts can possibly be. Consider spontaneous acts, like tying shoes or courteously opening doors for people. Such acts are habitual; they can be, to a spectator looking at them from the outside, moral or even immoral, but to the agent who acts spontaneously they are karma neutral. Kṛṣṇa is attempting to teach Arjuna the art of spontaneous, natural, karmaless action: Karma yoga.

Following the presentation of the description of karma yoga, Arjuna asks Kṛṣṇa what that person is like who has achieved mokṣa, who is liberated from saṁsāra, and who is a practitioner of spontaneous action. Kṛṣṇa in reply describes the karma yogi as the jīvanmukta, the person we have mentioned in our discussion of the *Upaniṣads* who is "liberated while still living." Notice that this jīvanmukta continues to act and live in the world and that he is not off in some isolated cave or forest retreat.

> When he abandons all desires that are in his heart, and finds satisfaction in himself, alone, then, Oh Arjuna, that one has truly reached steadfast wisdom.

> When in sorrow his mind is not disturbed, when he is indifferent to pleasures, when his passions, fears, and hatreds have departed, then he is called a holy man of steadfast mind.
>
> He who has no attachments toward anything, and who, having gotten this or that good or evil, neither delights in it nor hates it, then his mind is steadfast.[111]

The goal here is liberation, the production of the jīvanmukta; and karma yoga, we are told, will solve the dilemma of action and lead to liberation.

There is one other yoga hinted at in this same early chapter of the *Gītā,* a yoga that will receive greater treatment in the chapters that follow. It is mentioned in the context of the causes of bondage, in the inability to control the senses.

> For the churning senses can violently carry off even the mind of the most ardent striver for perfection.[112]

Kṛṣṇa describes in some detail the cause of bondage that originates from this inability to control the senses:

> When a man dwells on the objects of the senses, attachment to those objects is born. From this attachment desire is born and from [unfulfilled] desire hatred springs up.
>
> From this hatred comes obsession, and from obsession arises the loss of memory, and from the loss of memory arises the destruction of reason, itself. And from the destruction of reason, man, himself, is destroyed.[113]

And then the way out of this bondage to the uncontrolled senses is set forth. First, there is the control of the senses:

> But with desire and hatred severed, and with the senses, now controlled by the self, acting on the objects of the world, this self-controlled man attains true peace.
>
> In that peace all pains are extinguished; for such a man whose heart is peaceful his mind at last is steadfast.[114]

Second, there now appears that hint of another yoga that can lead to this same self-controlled condition:

> Restraining all his senses, let him sit, *his attention fixed on Me.* He whose senses are thus under control, his mind is steadfast.[115]

Fixing the attention on Kṛṣṇa Who, as events shortly reveal, is God, brings us to the second new yoga introduced in the *Gītā.* Let us have a brief look at this new way to peace, tranquility, and liberation, and a second way of breaking the dilemma of action.

Bhakti Yoga

The problems that Arjuna faces are the same problems as those stated in the dilemma of action, namely, bondage and saṁsāra. Having talked about karma yoga Lord Kṛṣṇa drops a hint that it would be useful if Arjuna fixed his attention "on Me." This hint will be expanded now into a full-fledged doctrine of bhakti yoga, the way of devotion to a personal God. Let us see what is going on here by beginning with a brief discussion of Hindu cosmology and the theory of creation.

The Hindus generally believe that *parā* (higher) Brahman causes the created universe of *aparā* (lower) Brahman to be brought into existence by parā Brahman's māyā. Now, aparā Brahman consists of all created entities from the Gods to man to animals to plants, rocks, oceans, and rivers. The Gods, in turn, consist of the Hindu trinity of Brahmā, the Creator of the worlds, Viṣṇu, the Preserver of the creation, and Śiva, the Destroyer, Who some day will bring the creation to an end. Following that ending and a period of rest, Brahmā will begin the process all over again. The cosmological periods are modelled, perhaps, after the cycle of the seasons. Time in the Hindu tradition, therefore, is conceived in terms of a cyclical model, rather than in terms of a linear model, as in the Judeo-Christian tradition.

Lord Kṛṣṇa as Savior

Into this cycle of creation comes the God Viṣṇu, the Preserver. Viṣṇu incarnates into the world from time to time to preserve or to reinstate righteousness. In the *Gītā* we see Viṣṇu in his current incarnation as the World Savior, Lord Kṛṣṇa. Of His origin Lord Kṛṣṇa has this to say:

> You and I have passed through many births, Arjuna; I know all of them but you do not.
>
> Though I am unborn and imperishable, though Lord of all beings, yet using my own nature, I come into existence using my own māyā.
>
> For whenever there is a decaying of dharma [righteousness, i.e., obedience to eternal and human laws], and a rising up of adharma then I send Myself forth.
>
> I come into existence time after time to protect the good, to destroy the wicked, and to reestablish the holy dharma.[116]

The Savior comes to earth after recognizing the wickedness present in the world. He or She or It preaches the message of salvation and then returns to the place from which He, She, or It came. There may be many such Āvatars or Descenders, as in Hinduism, or there may be only one, as in Christianity. The conclusion to this excursus into Āvatars and Saviors is that Lord Kṛṣṇa is in reality an incarnation of Lord Viṣṇu, that is, He is God and Savior, and, therefore, worthy of worship. And that worship is called "bhakti yoga."

One of the solutions to the dilemma of action, as we have seen, is to cease being attached to the consequences of actions. This liberates the agent from the karmic results of the action and leads eventually to liberation as the bonds of karma are sundered. Bhakti yoga works in a similar fashion. In utter devotion to God the *bhakta* ("devotee") surrenders everything to God including the desire for, and attachment to, the consequences of all action: Bhakti yoga *in this sense* is indistinguishable from karma yoga.

Bhakti yoga, like karma yoga, and unlike the yogas of the *Vedas* and the *Upaniṣads,* is a way to liberation that is open to all human beings. The truly universal appeal of the *Gītā* is found, once again, through the development of the doctrine of bhakti yoga. Lord Kṛṣṇa says:

> Arjuna, you must see that my devotees never perish. . . . For those who take refuge in Me, even though they are born from a womb of

> sin, even though they are women, vaiśyas, or even śūdras, they go to the highest goal.[117]

It may well be the case that bhakti yoga was designed especially for the two lower varṇas. But men and women from the two higher varṇas are invited to turn to bhakti yoga as well. Lord Kṛṣṇa continues:

> How much easier then for holy brahmins and devout royal seers [the kṣatriya varṇa is meant]. This is a fleeting and sorrowful world; while you are in it, lovingly dedicate yourself to Me.
>
> Fix your mind on Me; be dedicated to Me; lay yourself devotedly before Me; discipline yourself and with Me as your supreme goal, to Me you will surely come.[118]

The goal that the bhakta seeks is Lord Kṛṣṇa; the kind of liberation sought is fulfilled in utter and absolute identification with God:

> By bhakti he comes to know Me, what My measure is and Who I am in truth. Then having known Me truly he enters into Me immediately.[119]

This identification of the lover with the object of love means that the self no longer exists separately from God. Merged with God, the devotee and God are at-one. The actions performed by the devotee, therefore, are no longer the devotee's actions; rather, they are God's actions. Lord Kṛṣṇa now tells his beloved disciple the greatest secret of all. The following passages are surely the high points of aesthetic and linguistic elegance in all of the world's devotional literature:

> Listen once more to My supreme message, the greatest secret of all. You are truly my beloved and so I will tell you what is best for you.
>
> Merge your mind with Me, be my bhakta, sacrifice to Me, prostrate yourself before Me, and you shall come to Me. I promise this to you truly, for you are ever dear to Me.
>
> Abandoning all duties, come to Me alone for refuge. Be not sorrowed for I shall give you mokṣa from all sins.

> Mentally surrender all of your actions to Me, alone, intent on Me, alone, resorting to the yoga of the mind, have your thoughts now set on Me, alone.
>
> Thus focusing all your thoughts on Me, alone, you will overcome all problems by My grace. . . .[120]

The Savior Dilemma

A disturbing question arises at this point regarding the relation between the bhakta and God: Since God's grace or favor is so especially important to the bhakta and his liberation, can the bhakta, by engaging in the appropriate bhakti, force God to grant His grace? An interesting puzzle now develops; let us call it "the Savior dilemma:"

1. If I am devout (I engage in bhakti yoga) and this compels the Savior to forgive me (or grant me His grace or give me liberation, etc.) then the Savior is not *free* (the contradictory of "compelled").

2. If I am devout and this does not compel the Savior to forgive me then the Savior is capricious, i.e., inconstant.

3. Either my devotion compels the Savior to forgive me or it does not.

4. Therefore, either the Savior is not free or the Savior is capricious.

The Savior dilemma is a puzzle for any religion, such as Hinduism, Mahāyāna Buddhism, or Christianity, which urges that devotion can be a necessary and sufficient condition for grace or for forgiveness or for liberation or for whatever it is that devotees seek. The reader is left to ponder the Savior dilemma.

It would seem, then, that Lord Kṛṣṇa has promised Arjuna liberation, and it would also seem that we have at least two solutions to the dilemma of action: Karma yoga and bhakti yoga. However, two other more familiar yogas also receive favorable treatment in the *Bhagavad Gītā* and we shall turn to them next.

Dhyāna Yoga and Jñāna Yoga

If devotion to Lord Kṛṣṇa sounds familiar to us because of its similarity to our discussions about the kneeling devotions of the Indus Valley Harappāns, then it should come as no surprise that two other yogas, previously offered in the *Upaniṣads,* also receive treatment in the *Gītā.* And it should come as no surprise becaue we have suggested that the *Gītā* is attempting to blend these earlier Indian prescriptions for liberation and the traditions that they generated.

Dhyāna yoga is described in a brief but remarkably clear passage in the *Gītā.* In it Lord Kṛṣṇa teaches Arjuna the art of simple meditation (try it for yourself and see):

> Closing out all external objects, focusing the eyes between the eyebrows, making equal the inhalation and exhalation of the breath through the nostrils,
>
> The yogi who meditates with his senses, mind and reason controlled, who is intent on mokṣa and who has cast out desire, fear and anger, he is liberated forever.[121]

This passage is subsequently followed by a description of the physical and mental elements of dhyāna yoga:

> The yogi should practice ceaselessly to discipline his mind, seated in a quiet place, alone, controlled within and without, free from desires and possessions.
>
> In a pure place, let him sit on a firm seat that he has put there, neither too high nor too low, that has been covered with sacred kuśa grass, a deerskin, and a cloth.
>
> Sitting there let him make his mind concentrated on a single object with his thoughts and senses controlled, practicing yoga for the purification of the self.

> Let him sit holding the body, head and neck straight and steady, lifting his eyes up to the base of the nose, not letting them wander about.
>
> Let him sit with his self serene and without worry, firm in his vow of chastity, his mind under control, his thoughts on Me alone, intent on Me alone.
>
> The yogi with his mind thus under control attains to peace and ultimately to that supreme nirvāṇa ["liberation"] which rests in Me, alone.[122]

Thus dhyāna yoga in the *Gītā*.

But dhyāna, in addition to being a way to nirvāṇa, or mokṣa, is also a good psychological discipline that enables one to arrange one's life more appropriately by controlling the mind and getting it in order. The practice of meditational yoga, as millions of people have discovered, simply makes certain tasks easier and more enjoyable, tasks as varied as taking examinations and baking cakes.

Jñāna yoga, the second yoga handed down to the *Gītā* from the *Upaniṣads,* is familiar enough to us from our previous discussions. Here is Lord Kṛṣṇa discussing jñāna:

> Only through the destruction of ignorance by jñāna ["knowledge"], only by that will true knowledge shine forth like the sun, revealing the highest Self [Ātman].
>
> Thinking on That [Ātman], merging the self with That, making That the sole aim and object of their devotion, they reach a state from which there is no returning, their sins destroyed by true knowledge.[123]

The knowledge to which Lord Kṛṣṇa refers is, of course, the transcendental realization or mystical intuition of the nature of, and the identity between, one's true Self and Brahman, the knowledge that one is a Tiger and not a sheep.

The *Gītā* does not try to blend these four yogas into one kind of super yoga. In fact, there are passages that attempt not only to keep the yogas separate but also to rank them in terms of which one is better for Arjuna to follow. It is important to remember that Arjuna is a kṣatriya, that he does have a guṇa nature that consists of all three guṇas; however, we may suppose that for him rajas predominates over sattva and tamas in that nature, and that, ultimately, his appropriate yoga will be karma yoga. Here is Lord Kṛṣṇa recommending the various yogas available to Arjuna, discarding each one in turn in order to point to that one yoga most suitable to Arjuna's own personal nature, his *svabhāva*. First, two levels of concentration are recommended:

> Concentrate your mind completely on Me alone, let your reason enter into Me. Then in Me alone you will abide forever. Of this there is no doubt.
>
> But if you are not able to fix your mind on Me firmly, then seek to reach me instead by the repetition of less concentrated practice [*abhyāsa*].

If both of these deep and shallow methods of concentration should fail then the devotee is instructed to turn for help to God and to bhakti yoga:

> But if you are not able even by this concentration to reach Me, then do service for Me: perform actions for my sake alone.

If bhakti fails then there is always karma yoga.

> But if you are unable even to do thus then take refuge in my yoga: renounce the fruit of all action with the self under control.

Lord Kṛṣṇa then catalogues the various yogas and their appropriate order for Arjuna; notice that he mentions both jñāna and dhyāna yoga first:

> For jñāna is better than the practice of concentration; but better than jñāna is dhyāna; and better than dhyāna is the renunciation of the fruits of action [karma], for with renunciation there comes immediate peace.[124]

Thus Lord Kṛṣṇa's advice to Arjuna concludes with the recommendation that Arjuna seek salvation through karma yoga. But lest the reader or hearer believe that karma yoga is the only way to liberation, Lord Kṛṣṇa subsequently appends this passage:

> By dhyāna some perceive Ātman in the self by the self. Others by the yoga of knowledge; and others by karma yoga see Ātman.[125]

In other words, all yogas lead ultimately to liberation but some are more appropriate than others.

The *Bhagavad Gītā*

Let us turn now to the prescription for liberation from suffering and attempt to order and explain the philosophy and religion of the *Bhagavad Gītā.*

The Rx for Liberation from Suffering: The Bhagavad Gītā

The Problems

There are really two problems that the *Gītā* faces and attempts to solve. The first, which we might call "the Arjuna problem," is merely the problem of getting Arjuna to do his duty as a kṣatriya and to defend the right. In the last chapter of the *Gītā* Lord Kṛṣṇa asks Arjuna:

> Has what I have said been heard by you, Oh Arjuna, with single-minded attention? Has the delusion caused by ignorance in you been destroyed?

To which Arjuna answers:

> My delusion has been destroyed. I have gained recognition through your grace, Oh Changeless One [one of the many epithets of Kṛṣṇa used throughout the *Gītā*]. I stand firm with all my doubts fled. I shall act according to Your Word.[126]

And with that, although the *Gītā* does not describe it, Arjuna gathers up his arms and readies himself for the battle. The Arjuna problem is solved.

But the real problem, the philosophical problem, remains, and this is the problem of *duḥkha,* suffering. The word "duḥkha" appears some sixteen times throughout the *Gītā,* and the contexts in which it appears leave no doubt that it is the central problem of the *Gītā.* It is found in Arjuna's dilemma and it is found in the dilemma of action as Kṛṣṇa reminds Arjuna what will happen if he fails to do his duty:

> And many things that it would be improper to say to you, your enemies will say, slandering your honor. What now could lead to more duḥkha than that?[127]

Juxtaposed to this first alternative filled with duḥkha is a second alternative symbolized by the *muni,* a person of steady and tranquil mind (*sthitadhī*) who has gone beyond all duḥkha. It is this "muni-alternative," as we might call it, that is now dangled before Arjuna, an alternative, that can only come about if Arjuna does his duty:

> He whose mind is undisturbed though immersed in duḥkha, who is indifferent to sukha [pleasures], for whom all passions, fears and hatreds have departed, such a man is a muni of steady mind.[128]

Driven by the fear of unhappiness and attracted by the promise of happiness (liberation), Arjuna is at last brought to see that "delights are wombs of duḥkha,"[129] that "birth is the place of duḥkha,"[130] that the wise man is "not shaken by duḥkha"[131] for he sees that "everything is Ātman" and in so seeing he also "sees that sukha and duḥkha are ultimately the same."[132] Finally, the muni sees that "yoga destroys all duḥkha"[133] and that "yoga can break the chain of duḥkha."[134] The central choices here are suffering, the duḥkha-alternative, and its avoidance, the muni-alternative.

In the end, and given our previous discussion, we might say that the problem that the *Gītā* faces is duḥkha in this life and duḥkha in the next; for if the problem of duḥkha is not solved now, it will have to be solved when the self puts on another coat in the next life. In other words, duḥkha is saṁsāra in both senses, suffering and rebirth.

The Causes

The causes of suffering are two-fold: Kāma, desire or lust, and ajñāna, ignorance, though the *Gītā* adds another, *krodha,* hatred, which is reducible to desire, as we shall see.

Arjuna asks Lord Kṛṣṇa what it is that drives a man to do the evil (*pāpa*) that is bound to bring suffering and unhappiness in its wake. Lord Kṛṣṇa replies:

> It is lust [kāma], it is hatred [krodha], born of the guṇa of passion [rajas], all-devouring, all-polluting, that is the enemy, that is your real foe here on earth.
>
> Lust, the ever present enemy of the wise man [jñāni], envelopes true knowledge [jñāna] like an unquenchable fire.
>
> . . . Oh Great Arjuna, destroy this powerful enemy--lust.[135]

Two of these same causes of suffering are reiterated in the "three gates of hell" sermon preached by Kṛṣṇa as he warns Arjuna:

> These are the three gates of hell leading to the suffering [*nāśanam,* literally "destruction"] of the self: Lust, hatred and greed [lobha]. Therefore, let man renounce the three.[136]

Finally, a third cause of suffering is mentioned throughout the *Gītā* as Arjuna is repeatedly told to take on the qualities of the muni, the wise man or jñāni. This last cause of suffering, reflecting the Upaniṣadic heritage of the *Gītā,* is ignorance (ajñāna):

> Only through the destruction of ignorance [ajñāna] by true knowledge [jñāna], only by that will true knowledge shine forth like the sun, revealing the highest Self.[137]

We might well ask, How many causes of duhkha are there, and, for the sake of simplicity and elegance, could all the causes be reduced to one cause? Finally, we might ask, How would such a reduction of several causes (e.g., lust or desire, hatred, greed, and ignorance) to one cause, for example, ignorance, be carried out?

The most obvious first step in such a reduction would involve showing that hatred and greed are species of, or caused by, desire. For example, my hatred of an enemy is generally the result of some personal slight or injury that I wish or desire now to redress. If I was indifferent, that is, desireless, with regard to my "enemies," then I would, surely, have no enemies. Further, my greed is generally an excessive expression of my desire to possess something that I do not now possess or it is my desire to retain something that I do now possess. Thus this first reduction would show that desire is, indeed, my real enemy, and were I to conquer it, I would also, *pari passu*, have conquered hatred and greed.

The second reduction is a bit more tricky. It would entail reducing desire to a species of ignorance, and then arguing that conquering ignorance would be tantamount to conquering desire. But this reduction would entail assuming a rather Platonic doctrine, a doctrine that states that if a person knows the good then he or she will always do the good, and will, therefore, always be good. Plato of Athens (467-347 B.C.) had assumed that no one knowingly does evil, because to do evil is to hurt oneself, and no one would knowingly and willingly injure himself (the theory of psychological hedonism was not lost on Plato). Thus, for Plato, all evil, including lust and desire, is the result of ignorance. Were we to grant this Platonic assumption to the *Gītā,* the second reduction of desire to ignorance could easily be accomplished. But the *Gītā* is not prepared to accept that assumption.

The *Gītā* might well argue in the very opposite direction and claim that ignorance, far from having desire as one of its instances, is, in fact, an instance of desire. In other words, the *Gītā* might easily contend that if I were to eliminate or control or conquer desire, then ignorance would also be conquered. For example, my ignorance of my true Self or my ignorance of Brahman or my ignorance of where my highest happiness lies, it might be argued, is the result of my desire for other things than Self, Brahman, or highest happiness. If I was without desire for those other things and desired only the proper things (e.g., God, Lord Kṛṣṇa, or Brahman), then whether I was ignorant or not might be quite beside the point.

But because the matter is not clear with respect to this second reduction, and because the *Gītā* is loathe to make the Platonic assumption, and because both desire and ignorance play such strong and independent roles throughout the *Gītā* as causes of bondage and suffering, I am going to assume that both are distinct and irreducible causes of suffering. Therefore, the two causes of suffering are kāma and ajñāna.

The Solutions

The solution lies in mokṣa, "liberation" or "release." What one is released *from* is duḥkha, but what one is released *to* is ambiguous. Hinduism, like Buddhism, tends to speak of a dual solution to the problem of duḥkha. On the one hand, mokṣa can entail absorption into the Holy Power of the universe. The devotee disappears (i.e., the ego, personality, mind, memory, and consciousness of the devotee are assimilated), into Brahman. Following our discussion of Brahmanism of the *Upaniṣads,* let us call this "the absorption solution" to the problem of duḥkha.

On the other hand, mokṣa can entail the survival of the self in immortal and eternal bliss in the heavenly world of satisfied desires and undreamed-of delights in the presence of Lord Kṛṣṇa. Following our discussion of brahminism of the *Vedas,* let us call this "the heaven solution" to the problem of duḥkha. Borrowing from both the *Vedas* and *Upaniṣads,* and possibly from the Indus Valley Harappāns as well (remember those buried household implements and personal treasures in the Harappān graves), the *Bhagavad Gītā* advocates both an absorption solution as well as a heaven solution to the problem of duḥkha.

The heaven solution is clearly stated as Lord Kṛṣṇa invites his devotees to spend eternity with Him. He says to Arjuna:

> Merge your mind with Me, be My bhakta, sacrifice to Me, prostrate yourself before Me, and you shall come to Me. I promise this to you truly, for you are ever dear to Me.[138]

The absorption solution is also clearly stated in the *Gītā* in passages like the following:

> Thinking on That [highest Self], merging the self with That, making That the sole aim and object of their devotion, they reach a state from which there is no returning, their sins destroyed by true knowledge.[139]

The choices, as far as the solutions to the problem of duḥkha go, would seem to be, then, an eternity of unending peace, joy, and tranquility in the presence of a personal God such as Lord Kṛṣṇa, or absorption into Brahman with the total loss of personality and self-identity in the process.

The Ways

The *Gītā* introduces four yogas ("ways") for reaching the solution, whether heaven or absorption, to the problem. Let me briefly summarize these ways.

Karma Yoga

Karma yoga, "the way of action," offers a way out of the problem of suffering by showing the path to actionless action, that is, a way of acting that does not produce karmic consequences. In other words, karma yoga produces actions without karmic residues. And if an action is without karmic residues then the law of karma will not reward the agent (in a temporary heaven or by a better birth in the next life) nor will it punish the agent (in a temporary hell or by a worse birth in the next life). The conclusion is that the problem of suffering is solved because the cause of duḥkha, desire for the fruits of the act, is crushed by the yoga of actionless action, a yoga that leads ultimately to heaven and eternal peace in Lord Kṛṣṇa.[140]

Bhakti Yoga

Bhakti yoga, "the way of adoration," offers a way out of the problem of suffering by showing the path of selfless devotion to God. In other words, bhakti yoga also produces actions without karmic residues as the bhakta dedicates his actions and their consequences to an adored God; as a result, the karma generated by the act becomes God's and not the bhakta's. The conclusion is that the problem of suffering is solved once again, as the cause of duḥkha, desire, is crushed in the surrendering to God of all the fruits of one's labors. And, once again, the way to heaven is open.

Dhyāna Yoga

Dhyāna yoga, "the way of meditation," offers a way out of the problem of suffering that goes beyond the mere samādhi of the *Upaniṣads* by showing the path to the control of self and the discovery of Self through the control of breath. The use of a mantra, the burrowing into the center of the self in order to discover Ātman lying at that center, together with the results that follow such burrowing would seem to make dhyāna yoga similar in many respects to jñāna yoga. It may also be a good preliminary exercise to the successful practice of the other three yogas.

Jñāna Yoga

Jñāna yoga, "the way of knowledge," offers a way out of the problem of suffering by showing the path to the knowledge of Brahman. One comes to this knowledge by a kind of intuitive wisdom that reveals that the Ātman, the real Self within one's own self, is identical to Brahman. The knowledge of this identity between Ātman and Brahman produces immediate liberation. One is suddenly beyond the clutches of both good and bad karma. The law of karma that would reward or punish the agent of the action is rendered nugatory.

Jñāna yoga also "solves" the problem of suffering in a more radical way than either karma yoga or bhakti yoga. The latter two slipped between the horns of Arjuna's personal dilemma and the dilemma of action by suggesting that there was a third way of acting that was neither fighting nor not fighting *per se*; rather it was (by karma yoga) by acting but without desire or attachment to the results of whatever action one chose to do; or it was (by bhakti yoga) by acting but dedicating the action to God without desire or hope for reward for oneself. Both karma yoga and bhakti yoga were willing to focus attention on the act, both involved a skillful doing, and both were seeking to avoid karmic results through engaging in acts that were neither good nor bad but neutral with respect to those results.

But jñāna yoga calls for an entirely different approach. Strictly speaking, it does not *solve* the personal dilemma and the dilemma of action so much as it *dissolves* them. It does not involve one in action at all, but it invites, rather, a transcending of all action. It is the mystic's way to liberation; and the goal, following the *Upaniṣads* from which the yoga of jñāna comes, is not heaven but absorption into Brahman: One becomes That which one knows. The consequence is that the personal dilemma of action, as well as the problem of suffering, are both dissolved as ignorance is dispelled by jñāna and the Self merges with Brahman.

Table 3.2 **Guṇas and Yogas in the *Bhagavad Gītā***

Predominant Guṇa	Representative Varṇa	Appropriate Yoga	Expected Result	Escape from Saṁsāra?
Sattva	brahmin	jñāna-dhyāna	absorption	yes
Rajas	kṣatriya	karma	heaven	yes
Tamas	vaiśya	bhakti	heaven	yes
Tamas	śūdra, non-dvijas	bhakti	heaven	yes

We are now in a position to continue and complete Table 2.3, *Guṇas and Yogas in the Upaniṣads,* above.[141] Consider Table 3.2, which attempts to summarize the relation between the guṇas, varṇas, yogas, and the goals to which each yoga leads. Two things are noteworthy. First, the philosophy and religion of the *Bhagavad Gītā,* unlike either brahminism or Brahmanism, claim to provide a solution to the problem of saṁsāra for all Indians. In other words, the message of the prescription for liberation of the *Gītā* is truly pan-Indian as the escape from saṁsāra is now possible for all Indians, from brahmins to non-dvijas, from priests to śūdras, to untouchables and outcastes. Second, the philosophy and religion of the *Gītā* also claim that the expected results of yoga, either heaven or absorption, are also available to any person, whether he or she belongs to an Indian varṇa or not, provided only that that person applies the appropriate yoga to the right guṇa. In other words, the message of the prescription for liberation of the *Gītā* is truly universal as the escape from saṁsāra is now possible for all human beings, from Indians to Europeans, from Argentinians to Eskimos; one need only discover one's predominant guṇa nature and apply the appropriate yoga.

Guṇas, Varṇas, and Yogas

Examine once again the problem that faces us in the *Gītā* with respect to the yogas. The goal of human existence is still liberation or perfection. The way to that goal is yoga, and we have seen that there are four such yogas. Three of them, furthermore, are each appropriate to one particular guṇa nature. The fourth yoga, dhyāna, is appropriate as a possible preliminary to each of the other yogas, as well as being a bona fide way to liberation in and of itself. The guṇa nature one has is the result of one's previous life; one inherits one's guṇa nature from that previous life; and one's guṇa nature, finally, determines which varṇa one will be in. Now we can proceed back up through these statements, from varṇa to liberation, in the following summary way: If one knows one's varṇa, then one's guṇa nature is similarly known. If one's guṇa nature is known, then one's appropriate yoga is also known. If one's appropriate yoga is also known, then one can follow that appropriate yoga. If one follows that appropriate yoga, then one will eventually reach liberation. We can conclude from all of this: If one knows one's varṇa, then one can eventually reach liberation.

Now, as we've indicated, the Indians with their caste-class-occupational-varṇa society have or had little trouble discovering their varṇas and thereby satisfying the first condition of the above sorites (a chain of syllogistic arguments). But other societies and other cultures in other times and places have not been so fortunate. Where class and caste are known, of course, or where soul nature is knowable, there is no problem in discovering yogas or ways to the goal or goals of life. But knowing one's varṇa by the empirical method established by the Indians is surely, if all the other assumptions about the selves within that varṇa dharma system are correct, one of the most foolproof and obvious ways of discovering the nature of the self. I would like to mention another Indo-European self-discovery technique that roughly parallels the Indian scheme. This other technique is still used today, with some modifications, for classifying selves, hence it might give to us and other varṇaless, casteless drifters and seekers some insight into how we too might discover who we are, what our own guṇa nature is like, that we might also take up our appropriate yogas and travel the road to liberation and happiness. I want to introduce this second empirical technique, first introduced explicitly by Plato as a way for discovering who you are, what your soul nature is really like, and what you must do to find liberation from suffering.

Plato's Prescription for Liberation

Plato in his masterpiece called *Republic* sets out to establish a utopia ("utopia" can mean either "best place" [*eu-topos*] or "no place" [*ou-topos*]). He does this by banishing all adults from his society and then raising the children in accordance with certain programs of study. At various stages in this program there will be physical and mental examinations to determine whether or not the child or adolescent or young adult, man or woman, will go on to the next level or drop out. The drop-outs then take up the vocation or activity best suited to their natures or souls at that particular level. If they go on, they have a chance to learn, study, work, and live at more advanced levels, where further examinations (not necessarily written or oral) are expected and given. The citizens are being tested and categorized by their teachers in a fashion not unlike that carried out in contemporary social and educational environments.

Plato believed that his society would work for the benefit of all, and that happiness or liberation for all was possible, if the following four assumptions could be accepted:

1. Each person has one of three distinct soul natures.

This is the assumption that the *Bhagavad Gītā* has made, of course. Plato believed that people could be classified by the following three basic soul natures. The first was the *rational soul*; the intellectual and the thoughtful and the naturally contemplative person had this soul nature. The second was the *spirited soul;* the pugnacious and naturally active person had this soul nature. The third was the *appetitive soul;* the money-loving and gain-loving soul, and the naturally material-object-loving person had this soul nature. Plato assumed, furthermore, that each soul contained within itself parts of all three of these natures. In each soul, however, either its rational or its spirited or its appetitive part predominated, and that dominant part determined the soul nature of each individual. The parallel to the guṇa nature doctrine of the *Gītā* is striking, right down to and including Plato's belief in transmigration: One's present soul nature is a consequence of one's previous lives and is directly inherited from those previous lives.

Plato's assumption about the soul may not be as strange as it first looks. For example, in *The Wizard of Oz* by L. Frank Baum we meet a scarecrow, a lion, and a tin man who splendidly represent the three soul natures that Plato is discussing. Each of the three seeks the virtue appropriate to his calling in life, namely, wisdom, courage, and feeling, respectively. Baum (who, incidentally, was a devoted Theosophist) understood his Plato all too well. Moreover, many physiologists now suggest that the basic goals of modern Western society--knowledge or wisdom, honor or fame, and wealth or money--may be associated with a particular part of the brain, the site of modern man's "soul," the cerebral cortex, the motor centers, and the hind brain, respectively. Further, W. H. Sheldon has proposed that the three somatotypes, or body postures and physique--ectomorphy (thin), mesomorphy (muscular), and endomorphy (fat)--have corresponding mental or personality types to which they can be correlated, namely, cerebrotonia (brain-oriented), somatotonia (muscle-oriented), and viscerotonia (stomach-heart-oriented), respectively. What is shared by all of these parallels and symmetries from the humors of the time of Shakespeare to the current classifications of personalities in contemporary psychology is Plato's first assumption, that people have soul natures and that there are three such natures. His first assumption may not be as wild and unfamiliar as it initially seemed.

2. Whenever a person is living according to his soul nature, then he or she is happy.

If a man or a woman with a preponderance of the quality of reason in his or her soul is living and working at a vocation for which each is fitted by that soul quality, then each will be happy, i.e., liberated from suffering. At this point Plato joins three specific vocations to the three soul natures. Corresponding to the soul that is predominantly rational is the vocational class of the philosopher-kings, those fitted by their natures to rule, teach, and carry on the business of government. Corresponding to the soul that is predominantly spirited and active is the vocational class of the guardians and defenders, those fitted by their natures to protect and defend the people and the state. Finally, corresponding to the soul that is predominantly appetitive is the vocational class of the artisans, merchants, farmers, and peasants. Thus the vocational and social classes of the state are a direct result of the natures of the multiple selves or souls making up that state.

Socrates, the chief speaker in Plato's *Republic,* summarizes these findings to his friend Glaucon, pointing out that justice in the state as well as harmony and happiness in the soul come, in the end, to the same thing: each person and thereby each class doing what it is best fitted by its own nature to do.

> And so, after much tossing, we have reached land, and are fairly agreed that the same principles which exist in the State exist also in the individual, and that they are three in number.
>
> Exactly [Glaucon says].
>
> Must we not then infer that the individual is wise [and happy] in the same way, and in virtue of the same quality which makes the State wise?
>
> Certainly.
>
> Also that the same quality which constitutes courage in the State constitutes courage in the individual, and that both the State and the individual bear the same relation to all the other virtues?[142]

And Glaucon agrees. The other virtues that Socrates has in mind, which parallel the virtue of courage for the defender or soldier with a spirited soul, are wisdom for the soul of the philosopher-king and temperance or self-control for the artisan-merchant. Socrates had previously argued that each of the three soul natures, the rational, spirited, and appetitive, had a specific end or goal, a "virtue" that it pursued or ought to pursue, if it would be happy. The rational soul should seek and love wisdom; the spirited soul should seek and love honor; and the appetitive soul should seek and love gain; and these three ends become specific or particular for each type of soul. Socrates continues, with his friend Glaucon agreeing all the way:

> And the individual will be acknowledged by us to be just in the same way in which the State is just.

> That follows of course [Glaucon, again].
>
> We cannot but remember that the justice of the State consisted in each of the three classes doing the work of its own class?
>
> We are not very likely to have forgotten, he said.
>
> We must recollect that the individual in which the several qualities of his nature do their own work will be just, and will do his own work?
>
> Yes, he said, we must remember that too.
>
> And ought not the rational principle, which is wise, and has the care of the whole soul, to rule, and the passionate or spirited principle to be the subject and ally?
>
> Certainly.[143]

Socrates then describes the kind of education that is to be used in identifying the classes of souls and thereby the classes of men and women. In particular, music and gymnastics and subsequently mathematics and pure reasoning serve to select out the various classes. This brings us to the third assumption of Plato's *Republic.*

3. A person's specific soul nature can be empirically discovered.

Here is where the educational-selection process goes on, of course. Plato's educational plan was patterned somewhat as follows. Up through the age of fifteen years all citizens were to be taught reading, writing, music, the arts, and gymnastics. From fifteen to seventeen or eighteen years of age mathematics, the key to Plato's "higher education," was introduced. By the age of fifteen the few who were unsuited by nature to the higher education would begin to drop out. These were the artisans and farmers. By the age of seventeen still more would have fallen by the educational wayside, unsuited by nature for the roles of warrior or ruler-teacher-philosopher-king. From eighteen to twenty years of age, a strenuous course in military and physical training selected out the warrior-guardians. From twenty to thirty years, fewer still advanced on through the disciplines of the higher mathematics. From age thirty to thirty-five, fewer still were ready for the advanced work in dialectic and pure reasoning to train the intellect together with the theoretical study of advanced principles in morality. Finally, while those philosophers who fell by the wayside up to this point were fitted for lower levels of teaching, political, moral, social, and philosophic work, a very select few struggled on. From thirty-five to fifty years of age, these select few received practical in-service training in the business of running the state. At the age of fifty or thereabout these few became the aristocrats who reached the vision of the ultimate, mystical idea of the Good. Thereafter they devoted themselves to study and scholarship as philosophers, and ruled and directed the state as kings: These happy few became the philosopher-kings of Plato's great vision.

> Until philosophers are kings, or the kings and princes of this world have the spirit and power of philosophy, and political greatness and wisdom meet in one, and those commoner natures who pursue either to the exclusion of the other are compelled to stand aside, cities will never have rest from their evils--no, nor the human race, as I believe. . . .[144]

Unhappy states are the result of unhappy people who are the result of unhappy souls which are caused by people doing what is unnatural, i.e., what they are not fitted by their soul natures to do. The wrong people in the wrong jobs makes them unhappy, "unjust" in Plato's words, and they cause nothing but trouble for everyone else in the state. In a way, our modern educational system from our high schools to our vocational schools, to our colleges and universities, serve the same function today as Plato's schools were designed to serve his citizens: Education properly carried out helps each student to find his or her soul nature and to discover the vocation that each is fitted by that nature to pursue.

We come, finally, to the last of the assumptions of Plato's utopia.

4. Therefore, to be happy a person must discover and live according to his or her specific soul nature.

Here Plato's argument really ends: To be happy, to live well, let reason rule your soul, and find out for what vocation your soul nature best fits you. All men and women can be liberated or happy--the philosopher-king when he is wise; the guardian-defender when he is courageous; the artisan-farmer when he is self-controlled. And, Plato argues, only when reason rules the soul and guides the other two parts, the spirited and the appetitive, only when this kind of balance is maintained is the soul (or the state) happy (or just)--hence the importance of finding out who you are--what your soul nature is--so that your vocation can be adjusted to your soul nature. For man is only happy, liberated, when doing what he or she is fitted by nature to do. Thus Plato's prescription for liberation from suffering and Plato's way of discovering appropriate yogas.[145]

The Guiding Principle or Person: The Law of Karma and Lord Kṛṣṇa

The *Gītā* tells the sufferer that the prescription that has been given for solving the problem by treating the causes is guaranteed to work because the entire process is in the hands of an all-powerful Person or Principle. In general, that principle is the law of karma. And that Person is Lord Kṛṣṇa Himself.

Lord Kṛṣṇa possesses extraordinary powers, we are told, and it is these powers that seem to give Him the ability to annul the effects of karma, thereby making Him more powerful than the law of karma itself. Wendy Doniger O'Flaherty has stated the issue well and clearly:

> . . . devotion to God can overcome karma. This simple faith has an elaborate, classical foundation in the philosophy of Rāmānuja [eleventh century], who maintained that God could "even override the power of *karma* to draw repentant sinners to him." Thus the doctrine of karma is deeply determined by other important strains of Indian religion in which the individual is able to swim against the current of time and fate.[146]

For example, consider the nature of the promises that Kṛṣṇa is able to make to sorrowing Arjuna:

> Focusing all your thoughts on Me, you will be able to overcome all difficulties by My grace. . . .[147]

And again:

> Flee to Him alone for shelter with your entire being. By His grace you shall attain the highest peace and the eternal goal.[148]

And finally:

> Abandoning all dharma [duties] come to Me alone for refuge. Be not sorrowed for I shall give you mokṣa from all sins.[149]

Now several interesting questions and problems arise when one considers the relationships between an all-powerful law of karma and an all-powerful Lord Kṛṣṇa. Does Lord Kṛṣṇa grant His grace (*prasāda*), His forgiveness of sins, and His liberation *because of* the law of karma? In this case all of Kṛṣṇa's gracing, forgiving, and liberating would be superfluous, for liberation from suffering would have come automatically anyway, guaranteed by the law of karma, and without Kṛṣṇa's intervention. Or does Lord Kṛṣṇa grant his grace, forgiveness of sins and liberation from suffering, *in spite of* the law of karma? In this case all of Kṛṣṇa's gracing, forgiving, and liberating is truly a gift, a favor, a grace, and it is all done outside of, independently of, the law of karma. Let us call this little puzzle "the God-karma dilemma."

The God-karma dilemma concerns an argument about which, or who, is to be master here. Is Lord Kṛṣṇa more powerful than the law of karma in ending suffering and can He grant His devotees all that He claims that He can? Or is He as much a puppet in the hands of the law of karma as are the rest of us? Who is master here, Lord Kṛṣṇa or the law of karma? The God-karma dilemma can be stated more formally:

1. If the law of karma controls God then God is not omnipotent.

2. If God controls the law of karma then the law of karma is not a universal principle of justice.

3. Either the law of karma controls God or God controls the law of karma.

4. Therefore, either God is not omnipotent or the law of karma is not a universal principle of justice.

The God-karma dilemma, however it is resolved, necessitates our considering seriously the possibility that Lord Kṛṣṇa may be able to amend or abrogate the law of karma for his beloved devotees. Problems, puzzles, paradoxes, and dilemmas of the kind that we have been encountering here are bound to occur in any tradition that abounds in fertile, complicated, and clashing ideas. One has only to recall the history of Christian theology in the West and the ideological crises that occurred there over the divinity of Jesus, faith versus works, the theological problem of evil, human free will versus the omniscience or omnipotence of God, and so on, to see the truth of this assertion.

What has been said thus far about the prescription for liberation might be summarized for the *Gītā* as in Table 3.3.

Table 3.3 **The Rx for Liberation from Suffering: *The Bhagavad Gītā***

Problem:	Duḥkha as suffering
Causes:	Ajñāna (ignorance) and kāma (desire or lust)
Solution:	Mokṣa as either personal survival in heaven or as absorption into Brahman
Ways:	Dhyāna yoga and jñāna yoga lead to absorption; karma yoga and bhakti yoga lead to heaven
Guiding Principle or Person:	The law of karma and Lord Kṛṣṇa

Let me conclude our entire discussion of the *Gītā* by returning to the three philosophers with whom this brief introduction to Hinduism began. Let us now allow Mohandas Gandhi, Ramana Maharshi, and A. C. Bhaktivedanta to speak for themselves on the philosophy and religion of the *Gītā* as each interprets this most influential work. Preceding each presentation I shall offer some introductory observations about their statements and, following all three presentations, I shall conclude with some more general observations about Hinduism and the three quite distinct prescriptions for liberation represented by these philosophers.

Gandhi, Maharshi, and Bhaktivedanta on the Central Message of the *Bhagavad Gītā*

From what we have said previously in Chapter 1 about the three views of Mohandas Gandhi, Ramana Maharshi, and A. C. Bhaktivedanta, it should come as no surprise that their interpretations on so important a text as the *Bhagavad Gītā* will differ considerably. In the selections that follow, although each man states that all three yogas--karma yoga, jñāna yoga, and bhakti yoga--are presented in the *Gītā,* each man clearly shows a preference for only one of the yogas. Given our previous discussion on guṇas and yogas, the reasons for the preference should not be difficult to discover.

Gandhi on the Gītā

We turn to Mohandas Gandhi first, with a passage drawn from the introduction to his translation of the *Bhagavad Gītā.* In paragraphs 8-10 (paragraphs 1-7 are deleted from the selection) Gandhi defends the *Gītā* as an allegory as he locates the battle described in the *Gītā* as taking place in the human heart. The two heroes of the *Gītā* represent God or conscience, on the one hand, and self or ego, on the other. This interpretation is ingenious and goes a long way to explain the general appeal of the *Gītā* as a message for all beings of moral sensitivity and conscience; that is to say, for people who have ever been caught in a moral debate with themselves, Arjuna's dilemma and the dilemma of action, and Kṛṣṇa's solution to them, make a great deal of sense.

Second, in paragraphs 11-13, Gandhi discusses the belief that Kṛṣṇa is the incarnation of God. It is a curious discussion in several ways. Gandhi claims that Kṛṣṇa's perfection is "imagined," as is Kṛṣṇa himself, as the incarnation of perfection. Gandhi offers a naturalistic interpretation for the origin of Kṛṣṇa: Kṛṣṇa is merely one who was recognized by his own generation as "extraordinarily religious in his conduct." Kṛṣṇa possessed a spark of the divine within Himself; but so does everyone possess such a spark: In Kṛṣṇa the spark just happened to be brighter. Gandhi is obviously bothered by the attributions of Godness and perfection to a patently human and tribal hero such as Kṛṣṇa, and so he offers a psychological explanation for these all-too-divine attributions to Kṛṣṇa. Such attributions represent the restless human striving to become "like unto God," an ambition personified in the object called "Kṛṣṇa."

Third, paragraph 13 also introduces what Gandhi considers the aim of the *Gītā:* showing man the way to become "like unto God," that is, to self-realization.

Fourth, and finally, paragraph 14 indicates that the way is found through the renunciation of the fruits of action, through karma yoga. The remainder of this brief essay is merely an elaboration of this most important theme of karma yoga.

> 8. Even in 1888-89, when I first became acquainted with the *Gita,* I felt that it was not a historical work, but that, under the guise of physical warfare, it described the duel that perpetually goes on in the hearts of mankind, and that physical warfare was brought in merely to make the description of the internal duel more alluring. This preliminary intuition became more confirmed on a closer study of religion and the *Gita.* A study of the *Mahabharata* gave it added confirmation. I do not regard the *Mahabharata* as a historical work in the accepted sense. The *Adiparva* [first book of the *Mahabharata*] contains powerful evidence in support of my opinion. By ascribing to the chief actors superhuman or subhuman origins, the great Vyasa made short work of the history of kings and their peoples. The persons therein described may be historical, but the author of the *Mahabharata* has used them merely to drive home his religious theme.
>
> 9. The author of the *Mahabharata* has not established the necessity of physical warfare; on the contrary he has proved its futility. He has made the victors shed tears of sorrow and repentance, and has left them nothing but a legacy of miseries.

10. In this great work the *Gita* is the crown. Its second chapter, instead of teaching the rules of physical warfare, tells us how a perfected man is to be known. In the characteristics of the perfected man of the *Gita*, I do not see any to correspond to physical warfare. Its whole design is inconsistent with the rules of conduct governing the relations between warring parties.

11. Krishna of the *Gita* is perfection and right knowledge personified; but the picture is imaginary. That does not mean that Krishna, the adored of his people, never lived. But perfection is imagined. The idea of a perfect incarnation is an aftergrowth.

12. In Hinduism, incarnation is ascribed to one who has performed some extraordinary service of mankind. All embodied life is in reality an incarnation of God, but it is not usual to consider every living being an incarnation. Future generations pay this homage to one who, in his own generation, has been extraordinarily religious in his conduct. I can see nothing wrong in this procedure; it takes nothing from God's greatness, and there is no violence done to Truth. There is an Urdu saying which means, "Adam is not God but he is a spark of the Divine." And therefore he who is the most religiously behaved has most of the divine spark in him. It is in accordance with this train of thought, that Krishna enjoys, in Hinduism, the status of the most perfect incarnation.

13. This belief in incarnation is a testimony of man's lofty spiritual ambition. Man is not at peace with himself till he has become like unto God. The endeavor to reach this state is the supreme, the only ambition worth having. And this is self-realization. This self-realization is the subject of the *Gita*, as it is of all scriptures. But its author surely did not write it to establish that doctrine. The object of the *Gita* appears to me to be that of showing the most excellent way to attain self-realization. That which is to be found, more or less clearly, spread out here and there in Hindu religious

books, has been brought out in the clearest possible language in the *Gita* even at the risk of repetition.

14. *That matchless remedy is renunciation of fruits of action.*

15. This is the centre round which the *Gita* is woven. This renunciation is the central sun, round which devotion, knowledge and the rest revolve like planets. The body has been likened to a prison. There must be action where there is body. Not one embodied being is exempted from labour. And yet all religions proclaim that it is possible for man, by treating the body as the temple of God, to attain freedom. Every action is tainted, be it ever so trivial. How can the body be made the temple of God? In other words, how can one be free from action, i.e., from the taint of sin? The *Gita* has answered the question in decisive language: "By desireless action; by renouncing fruits of action; by dedicating all activities to God, i.e., by surrendering oneself to Him body and soul."[150]

Maharshi on the Gītā

Ramana Maharshi's interpretation of the *Gītā* goes along an entirely different path. Let me begin, as before, by making several introductory comments.

First, the introductory paragraph and title that appear below were both provided by Maharshi's editor, Arthur Osborne. This paragraph explains the source of the 42 out of 700 verses that Maharshi had designated as containing the essence of the *Gītā*. The jñāna yoga bias of the 42 verses, and the portions of them that I quote below, is obvious.

Second, in verse 1 we find Arjuna full of despair and confusion, awaiting Kṛṣṇa's answer to his anguished questions. The verse is important because it reminds Maharshi's readers or listeners that Kṛṣṇa is not speaking into the empty wind but rather to human beings who have problems, who are suffering, and who are devoured by anxiety.

Third, in verses 2 to 4, Maharshi, like Gandhi, launches into a description (quoting the *Gītā*) of the place, the *kṣetra* or field, where the great battle is to be fought and where the problems that led to it are to be solved: The place or field is the body; therefore, the Self and the Knower of the field are going to be in the body as well.

Fourth, for the sake of brevity I have eliminated verses 5 through 17, but in them the Self or He is identified with That, i.e., with Brahman, the Holy Power of the universe. The eliminated verses are nothing more than injunctions by Kṛṣṇa to Arjuna to know this Self, the That that is beyond description.

Fifth, the remainder of the 42 key verses, of which several are quoted below, are an elaboration of this theme of knowing the Self, knowing Brahman. Passages where bhakti yoga is mentioned (verses 18, 32, and 33) or passages where karma yoga is mentioned (verse 39) are there, as Maharshi makes clear, merely as supports for, or as the effects of, jñāna yoga. All of the emphasis is on knowledge and knowing the Self in an endeavor to answer that most important question that the *Upaniṣads* asked, that Plato asked, and that the *Gītā* now asks: Who am I?

The Song Celestial

> Bhagavan [Maharshi] was speaking once with a visiting pandit about the great merits of the Bhagavad Gita, when a devotee complained that it was difficult to keep all the 700 verses in mind and asked if there was not one verse that could be remembered as the quintessence of the Gita. Bhagavan thereupon mentioned Book X, verse 20: 'I am the Self, Oh Gudakesa, dwelling in the Heart of every being; I am the beginning and the middle and also the end of all beings.' Then he selected [the verses] that here follow (of which that just quoted was the fourth). . . .

* * * * * *

Sanjaya said:

1. To him (Arjuna) thus filled with compassion and in despair, his eyes distressed and full of tears, spoke Madhusudana [Lord Kṛṣṇa] these words:

The Blessed Lord said:

2. This body, Oh son of Kunti, is called the *kshetra* (Field); Him who know it, the Sages call, the *kshetrajna* (Knower of the Field).

3. Know Me also as the Knower of the Field in all the Fields, Oh Bharata: knowledge of the Field and of the Knower of the Field I deem to be true Knowledge.

18. He that has intense faith, and to that faith being devoted has the senses controlled, gains Knowledge; and having gained Knowledge he swiftly attains Supreme Peace.

20. Out of compassion for them and abiding in their Self I destroy with the resplendent Light of Knowledge their darkness born of ignorance.

21. In those in whom ignorance is destroyed by Knowledge of the Self, Knowledge like the sun illumines That Supreme.

24. Just as a burning fire makes ashes of its fuel, Oh Arjuna, even so does the Fire of Knowledge make ashes of all works.

25. Him whose every enterprise is without desire or motive, whose actions are burnt up in the Fire of Knowledge, the wise call a Sage.

32. Of these the *Jnanim* who is ever attuned, whose devotion is centred in One, is the most excellent; because to the *Jnani* I am exceedingly dear and he is dear to Me.

33. At the end of many births the *Jnani* finds refuge in Me, recognizing that Vasudeva is all. Such a high Soul is very hard to find.

> 34. When one puts away, Oh Partha, all the desires that are in the mind, and in the Self alone, by the Self, is well satisfied, then is one called a man of steadfast Wisdom.
>
> 38. The man who revels here and now in the Self alone, with the Self is satisfied, and in the Self alone is content--for him there is no work to do.
>
> 39. For him there is no purpose either in doing work or in leaving it undone; nor is there in all beings anything which serves him as a purpose.[151]

Bhaktivedanta on the Gītā

Swami Bhaktivedanta's interpretation of the *Gītā* takes a different tack entirely from either Gandhi's or Maharshi's. Nowhere is this difference more apparent than in Bhaktivedanta's translation of and interpretation of the *Bhagavad Gītā*. Let me begin, as before, by making several introductory comments.

First, as one would expect, for Bhaktivedanta the *Gītā* is primarily a bhakti text, expressing Lord Kṛṣṇa's love for man with the expectation of a return of that love to Lord Kṛṣṇa. In good Fundamentalist Kṛṣṇaism fashion, and after warning the reader against the "so-called scholars" who "push forward their demonic propensities and mislead people regarding right understanding,"[152] Bhaktivedanta charges that the "absolute position of Kṛṣṇa is difficult to understand for any person who is not a devotee of Kṛṣṇa in the *paramparā* (disciplic succession) system."[153] Being in that succession himself he is able, he states, to offer the "authorized" commentary and the "authorized translation":

> To interpret *Bhagavadgītā* without any reference to the will of Kṛṣṇa is the greatest offense. In order to save oneself from this offense, one has to understand the Lord as the Supreme Personality of Godhead. . . .[154]

It is this understanding then that allows Bhaktivedanta to express the central message of the *Gītā:*

> This is the art, and this is also the secret of *Bhagavadgītā:* total absorption in the thought of Śrī Kṛṣṇa.[155]

Such absorption and the means of attaining it is what bhakti yoga is all about.

Second, the other yogas of the *Gītā* when they are treated or practiced in isolation from bhakti become insignificant; and they become significant only when they are interpreted as adjuncts to the only important yoga of the *Gītā:* Bhakti yoga.

In this regard it is interesting to see how Bhaktivedanta defines "jñāna-yoga" and "karma-yoga." In a sense, these other two yogas lose in the struggle for significance even before the game is begun. For not only are the good Swami's definitions contrary to the accepted and popular definitions of these concepts within the Hindu tradition that we have been developing in this brief text, but each definition contains within itself, so to speak, the pejorative seeds of its own destruction:

> *Jñāna-yoga* - the predominantly empirical process of linking with the Supreme, which is executed when one is still attached to mental speculation.[156]

This is not, of course, the jñāna yoga of either the *Upaniṣads* or the Upaniṣadic tradition represented by Ramana Maharshi. In that tradition jñāna is neither empirical nor speculative; rather it is intuitional and certain. Bhaktivedanta continues:

> *Karma-yoga* - (1) action in devotional service; (2) action performed by one who knows that the goal of life is Kṛṣṇa but who is addicted to the fruits of his activities.[157]

This is not, of course, the karma yoga of either Mohandas Gandhi or the *Gītā* as Gandhi interprets it. The first definition is loaded in favor of bhakti, a loading confirmed by the second definition. Further, the second definition of "karma yoga" makes all karma yogis addicts to fruits of actions when, as we have seen above, the very purpose of karma yoga is precisely to overcome such addiction. Finally, the second definition ties all karma yoga actions to both Lord Kṛṣṇa and from that, by implication, to bhakti yoga, a tying that is grossly unfair given the karma yoga tradition we have been examining above.

To make his case, one strategy adopted by Bhaktivedanta is to represent all yogas other than bhakti as inferior.

> The culmination of all kinds of yoga practice lies in *bhakti-yoga*. All other yogas are but means to come to the point of *bhakti* in *bhakti-yoga*....
>
> If one is fortunate enough to come to the point of *bhakti-yoga*, it is to be understood that he has surpassed all the other *yogas*. Therefore, to become Kṛṣṇa conscious is the highest stage of yoga. . . .[158]

Another strategy lies in representing other yogas as simply techniques climaxing in bhakti.

> Yoga actually means *bhakti yoga;* all other *yogas* are progressions toward the destination of *bhakti-yoga*. . . . [159]

Third, in arguing that the *Gītā* is ultimately and only a bhakti text, Bhaktivedanta must alter, retranslate, or reinterpret a great number of passages in the *Gītā*. That is to say, to make his point it is incumbent upon him to take obvious karma yoga and bhakti yoga passages, passages that we have already noted in Gandhi and Maharshi above, and torture them a bit either by translation or interpretation in order to get them to come out as bhakti passages.

The culmination of all of the above is reached in Bhaktivedanta's actual translation of and commentary on the *Gītā*. It is interesting to compare passages in other translations of the *Gītā* with those of Bhaktivedanta to note the curious and oftentimes embarrassing discrepancies.

In one famous and genuine karma yoga verse of the *Gītā* Kṛṣṇa tells Arjuna that mere action is inferior to the discipline of detached action ("buddhi yoga"); seek your refuge in that detachment, he is told. Bhaktivedanta, by rendering "buddhi yoga" as "on the strength of Kṛṣṇa consciousness" translates the verse as:

> O Dhanaṁjaya, rid yourself of all fruitive activities by devotional service, and surrender fully to that consciousness.[160]

Gandhi's rendering is as follows:

> For action, O Dhanaṁjaya, is far inferior to unattached action; seek refuge in the attitude of detachment.[161]

Gandhi's rendering of the next verse is:

> Here in this world a man gifted with that attitude of detachment [*buddhiyukta*] escapes the fruit of both good and evil deeds.[162]

which Bhaktivedanta translates as:

> A man engaged in devotional service rids himself of both good and bad actions in this life.[163]

"Devotional service" to Lord Kṛṣṇa, a bhakti activity, certainly, is derived from a passage that contains no mention of "bhakti" at all.

In genuine jñāna passages that focus on the impersonality of Ātman and the Highest, Bhaktivedanta interprets the passages so as to give them a distinctively bhakti flavor. In Chapter 5 we have the following, which I translate quite straightforwardly as:

> Only through the destruction of ignorance by knowledge [*jñāna*] of the Ātman, only by that will true knowledge [*jñāna*], revealing the Highest [*parā*], shine forth like the sun.
>
> Thinking on That [*tat,* a neuter pronoun], merging the Ātman with That, making That the sole aim and object of their efforts, they reach a state from which there is no returning, their sins dispelled by true knowledge [*jñāna*].[164]

Bhaktivedanta comments on these verses from his own translation, pointing out that the center of the Highest contains the personality of Lord Kṛṣṇa:

> The Supreme Transcendental Truth is Lord Kṛṣṇa. The whole *Bhagavad-gītā* centers around the declaration of Kṛṣṇa as the Supreme Personality of Godhead.[165]

On the other hand, for Maharshi, as we have seen, the *Bhagavad Gītā* centers around the Supreme *Im*personality of Godhead, and that neuter pronoun, *tat,* is about as impersonal as the Sanskrit can possibly get.

Here then is Swami Bhaktivedanta's rendering of the central message of the *Bhagavad Gītā:*

> 1. Arjuna said [to Lord Kṛṣṇa]: You are the Supreme Brahman, the ultimate, the supreme abode and purifier, the Absolute Truth and the eternal Divine Person. You are the primal God, transcendental and original, and you are the unborn and all-pervading beauty.[166]
>
> 2. Anyone who quits his body, at the end of life, remembering Me, attains immediately to My nature; and there is no doubt of this.[167]
>
> 3. Therefore, Arjuna, you should always think of Me, and at the same time you should continue your prescribed duty and fight. With your mind and activities always fixed on Me, and everything engaged in Me, you will attain to Me without any doubt.[168]
>
> 4. Of all *yogis,* he who always abides in Me with great faith, worshipping Me in transcendental loving service, is most intimately united with Me in yoga, as is the highest of all.[169]
>
> 5. By practicing this remembering [of Lord Kṛṣṇa], without being deviated, thinking ever of the Supreme Godhead, one is sure to achieve the planet of the Divine, the Supreme Personality.[170]
>
> 6. O son of Pārtha, anyone who will take shelter in Me, whether a woman, or a merchant, or one born in a low family, can yet approach the supreme destination. How much greater then are the *brāhmaṇās,* the righteous, the devotees, and saintly kings! In this miserable world, these are fixed in devotional service to the Lord.[171]

> 7. Give up all varieties of religiousness, and just surrender unto Me; and in return I shall protect you from all sinful reactions. Therefore, you have nothing to fear.[172]

Bhaktivedanta ends this discussion of the bhakti spirit of the *Gītā* by stating:

> In this present day, man is very eager to have one scripture, one God, one religion, and one occupation. So let there be one common scripture for the whole world - *Bhagavad Gītā.* And let there be one God only for the whole world - Śri Kṛṣṇa. And one *mantra* only - Hare Kṛṣṇa, Hare Kṛṣṇa, Kṛṣṇa Kṛṣṇa, Hare Hare / Hare Rāma, Hare Rāma, Rāma Rāma, Hare Hare. And let there be one work only - the service of the Supreme Personality of Godhead.[173]

Conclusion

The uniqueness and universality of the *Gītā* lay in its ability to blend these three traditions, the Vedic tradition, which Gandhi finds in the *Gītā,* the Upaniṣadic tradition, which Maharshi finds in the *Gītā,* and the devotional tradition, which Bhaktivedanta finds in the *Gītā*, into a single, coherent prescription for liberation. It is coherent in the logical sense for it is consistent in that none of the prescriptions for liberation appear to contradict each other; and it is coherent in the semantical sense in that the language in which the prescriptions for liberation are presented seems clear and without muddles. The *Gītā* is simply saying that all three traditions, and perhaps many more as well, are right and that they are right relative to karma yogis, to jñāna yogis, and to bhakti yogis, i.e., relative to yogis such as Gandhi, Maharshi, and Bhaktivedanta. We turn next to several final observations about Hinduism as seen through the prescription for liberation from suffering for bhaktism, brahminism, and Brahmanism.

4

Some Concluding Observations on Hinduism: Bhaktism, Brahminism, and Brahmanism

Let me conclude this brief discussion of Hinduism by doing two things. First, I will summarize the results of our investigations into the prescription for liberation from suffering for the Harappans, the *Vedas*, the *Upaniṣads*, the *Bhagavad Gītā*, Mohandas Gandhi, Ramana Maharshi, and A. C. Bhaktivedanta; and second, I will answer the question with which this entire investigation began, namely, How could these three Hindus--Gandhi, Maharshi, and Bhaktivedanta--offer such diverse solutions to the religious and philosophic problems of Hinduism, solutions that seem so patently opposed to one another, and still be called Hindus? In other words, How can three Hindus hold views about philosophy and religion, views about the prescription for liberation from suffering, that *seem* to be so opposed to, if not inconsistent with, one another?

Below, in Table 4.1, is the summary of the previous tables for the Rx for liberation from suffering relating to the traditions, texts, and persons of Hinduism. The three Hindu traditions about which we spoke previously--brahminism, Brahmanism, and bhaktism--are clearly expressed in Table 4.1.

Table 4.1 The Rx for Liberation from Suffering: Hinduism

	Harappāns	*Vedas*	*Upaniṣads*
	(bhaktism)	(brahminism)	(Brahmanism)
Problem:	Possibly, suffering as concern about life after death and anxiety over survival and prosperity now	Suffering: Anxiety about getting wealth in this world and heaven in the next	Saṁsāra as suffering in this world and rebirth in the next
Causes:	Possibly, realizing that certain external and natural forces are threatening and uncontrollable	Disobedience and neglect of the eternal laws and the ritual sacrifice	Avidyā (ignorance), the chief cause, and kāma (desire), the secondary cause
Solution:	Possibly, achieving a better life after death and attaining power over those threatening forces	Achieving the power to obtain heaven	Mokṣa as mystical absorption and release from saṁsāra
Ways:	Possibly, propitiating the Gods and the forces of nature through bhakti yoga	Leading a moral life and paying attention to the Gods through action, i.e., prayer and sacrifice	Dhyāna yoga (to samādhi) and jñāna yoga (to mokṣa)
Guiding Principle or Person:	Unknown, though possibly associated with some Power or personal God in nature	Ṛta and, among others, Lord Varuṇa	The law of karma

Table 4.1, continued

Bhagavad Gītā	M. Gandhi	R. Maharshi	A. C. Bhaktivedanta
(Hinduism)	(brahminism)	(Brahmanism)	(bhaktism)
Duḥkha as suffering	Suffering of others	One's own suffering	Suffering in oneself and others
Ajñāna (ignorance) and kāma (desire or lust)	Selfishness, social problems, British occupation, etc	Ignorance of Self	Indifference to, or ignorance of, Kṛṣṇa
Mokṣa as either absorption into Brahman or personal survival in heaven	self-realization	Self-realization	Kṛṣṇa-realization
Dhyāna yoga and jñāna yoga (to Brahman), karma yoga and bhakti yoga (to heaven)	Karma yoga and satyagraha	Jñāna yoga, be still	Bhakti yoga by meditation and kīrtana
The law of karma and Lord Kṛṣṇa	God, the law of karma	Brahman, the law of karma	Lord Kṛṣṇa

Recall that brahminism has its origin in the *Vedas* and that it finds a later formulation in one of the three views expressed in the *Bhagavad Gītā*. In brahminism the stress is placed upon three things: First, righteous action (e.g., not sinning against the Gods or man); second, sacrifice (e.g., ritual action in the *Vedas* and karma yoga in the *Gītā*); and third, concern for the Gods (e.g., propitiation of Varuṇa in the *Vedas*). In brahminism, furthermore, emphasis is placed upon personal survival in an eternal heaven after death, as in the *Vedas*, or personal survival in an eternal heaven with Lord Kṛṣṇa after liberation, as in the *Gītā*. Brahminism, finally, appears to rest upon a metaphysical pluralism, which holds that there are many real entities in the universe, including many real Gods and many real selves.

Recall that Brahmanism has its origin in the *Upaniṣads* and that it, too, finds a later formulation in one of the three views expressed in the *Bhagavad Gītā*. In Brahmanism the stress is placed upon three things: First, jñāna yoga and the knowledge of the mystical identity that obtains between immanent Ātman and transcendent Brahman; second, the utter impersonality and guṇaless character of both Ātman and Brahman; third, knowledge that one's Self is Brahman leads to liberation and absorption of the liberated Self into Brahman as both the *Upaniṣads* and the *Gītā*, again, make clear. In Brahmanism, furthermore, emphasis is placed upon the nonsurvival of a personal self after liberation since only Self is real and self is not. Brahmanism, finally, rests upon a metaphysical monism, which holds that there is only one real entity in the universe--Brahman (or Ātman or Self).

Recall that bhaktism probably has its origin in one or more of the indigenous or native ancient and prehistoric cults of India, cults that probably go back as far as the Indus Valley civilization of the third millennium B.C.E. These native cults were devoted to non-Āryan deities, such as the later Śiva and Kṛṣṇa, and to the worship of the Gods and Goddesses of fertility, trees, ponds, and other natural elements and forces. The *Bhagavad Gītā* is in part but one of many expressions of this love for and attachment to a personal God by adoring and dedicated suppliants. In bhaktism the stress is placed upon three things: First, bhakti yoga and the utter devotion of the bhakta to the loving and personal God; second, the God who is sought by the bhakta is a Person capable of acting like a loving and forgiving Parent or Friend toward His or Her beloved worshipper; third, personal and eternal survival of the bhakta in heaven in close eternal contact with the loving God. Bhaktism, finally, rests upon a kind of metaphysical pluralistic monism, which holds that while Kṛṣṇa alone is ultimately and absolutely real His beloved disciples may share in that reality in loving devotion to Him.

From what has been said thus far, it should be apparent that Mohandas Gandhi followed the traditions of brahminism more than he followed the tradition of Brahmanism or bhaktism. Just as moral and sacrificial acts were the keys to solving the problem of suffering in the *Vedas,* and just as karma yoga holds the key to liberation as one of the three views expressed in the *Gītā,* so also for Gandhi, as for Arjuna, it is proper action that will end suffering and cure the woes of the world and guarantee either a better birth or a heavenly crown in the next world for the active moral agent. Gandhi's repeated stress on karma yoga, or action without desire, in his philosophy of satyagraha supports the claim that he was one of the world's most prominent exponents and practicers of karma yoga and brahminism.

From what has been said thus far, it should be equally apparent that Ramana Maharshi followed the tradition of Brahmanism more than he followed the tradition of brahminism or bhaktism. Just as *being still* was the key to the dhyāna and jñāna yogas of the *Upaniṣads,* so also for Maharshi it is being still and discovering the Self in the quiet depths of meditation that will end ignorance and suffering in the world. Maharshi's repeated stress on jñāna yoga, the knowledge of the Self, and his philosophy of silence supports the claim that he was one of the world's most prominent exponents and practicers of jñāna yoga and Brahmanism.

Finally, from what has been said thus far, it should be equally apparent that A. C. Bhaktivedanta followed the tradition of bhaktism. In fact, as we have seen, he rejected both brahminism and Brahmanism as ways to his beloved Kṛṣṇa. Insofar as brahminism and Brahmanism have any currency at all for Bhaktivedanta, they would be of use only after bhaktism itself had been allowed to have full expression. Selfless action and intuitive knowledge, in other words, have meaning in the context of bhaktism only as useful supports of, or as natural results of, loving devotion to Lord Kṛṣṇa.

The question with which we began our investigation of Hinduism appears to be answered, for things are not always what they seem. Three men, all Hindus, can hold opposing views about the way to solve the problem of suffering precisely *because* all three men *are* Hindus, and "opposition" does not mean "contradiction." For it is one of the basic assumptions of Hinduism that there are at least three equally right views about the ways to end human suffering. That assumption is graphically illustrated, as we have seen, in the very foundations of Hinduism: In the Indus Valley civilization, in the *Vedas,* and in the *Upaniṣads* as well as in the *Bhagavad Gītā* where all three views are skillfully and coherently intertwined in one of the greatest religious texts known to the world. Again, no one of the prescriptions for liberation is better than the others. Instead, each prescription is simply more appropriate or less appropriate to the individual guṇa natures of the men and women caught up in the world's suffering, pain, and agony.

Appendix A:
Three Hindu "Saints": Mohandas Gandhi, Ramana Maharshi, and A. C. Bhaktivedanta

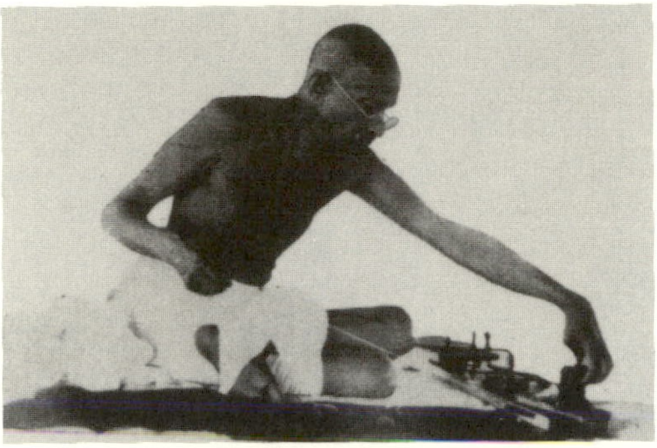

Mahatma Mohandas K. Gandhi
(1869-1948)
AT THE SPINNING WHEEL

Bhagavan Śri Maharshi
(1879-1950)

Swami A. C. Bhaktivedanta
(1896-1977)

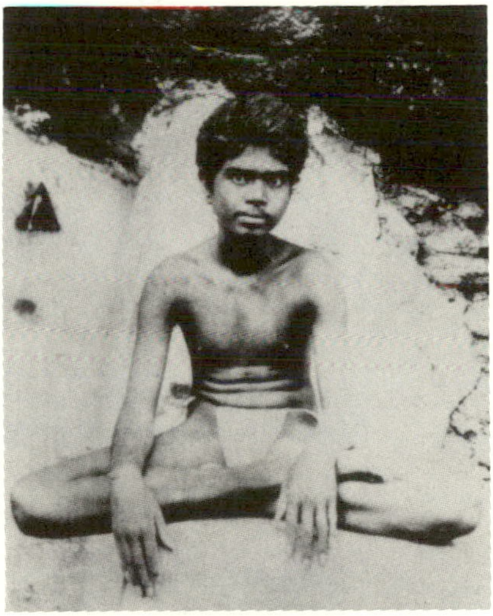

Ramana Maharshi at age 21.
Five years after his liberation.

Appendix B: Indus Valley (Mohenjodaro) and Modern Materials

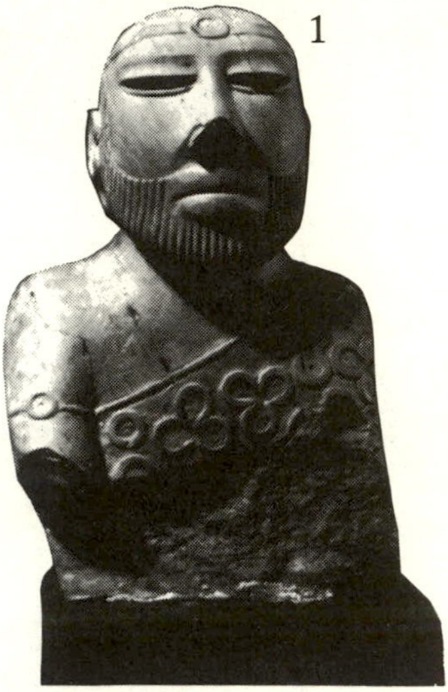

1

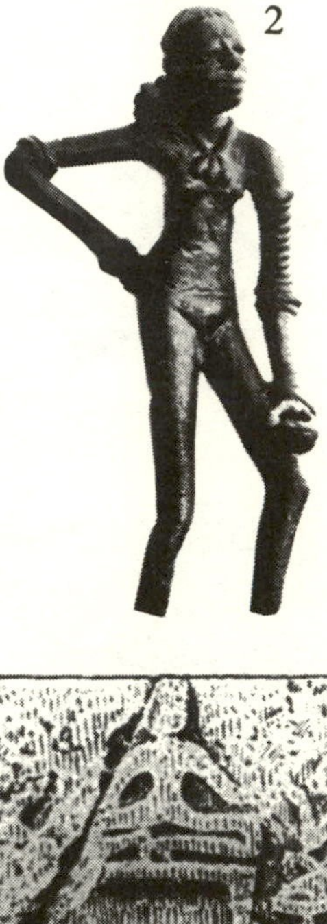

2

3

4

5

6

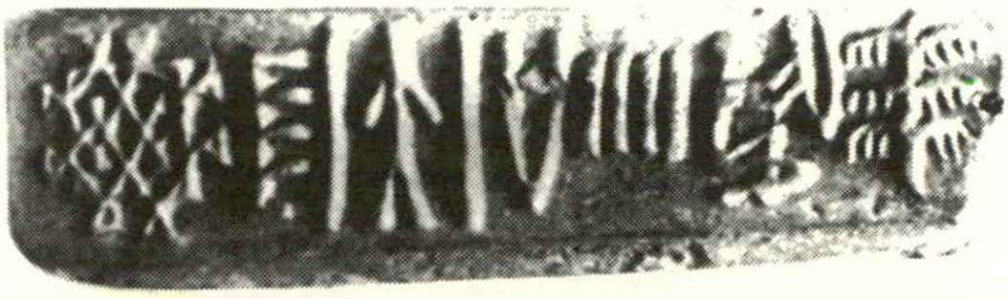

8a

8b

7

9

10

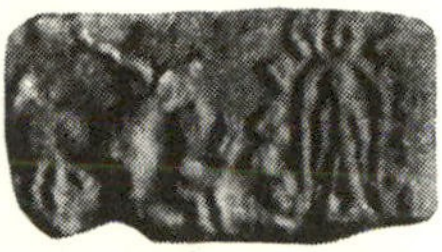

11

12

13

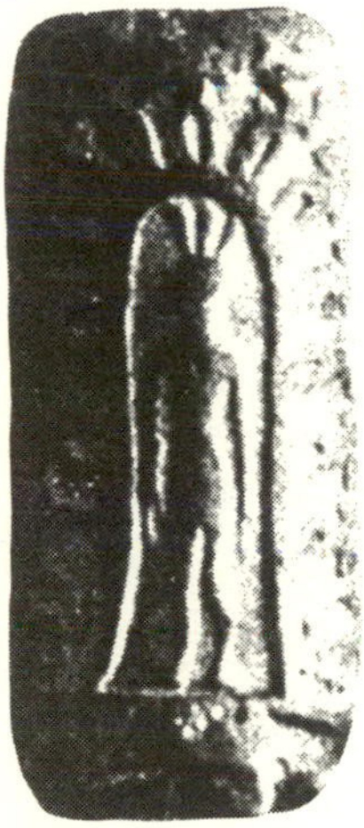

14

15

Descriptions of Sculptures and Stamp Seals (see pp. 41-43)

1. Bust of Bearded Man
2. Bronze "Dancing Girl"
3. Seal of a Bull with "Ritual Altar"
4. Figure in "Lotus-posture" with Serpents and Worshippers
5. Figure in "Lotus-posture"
6. Śiva Figure (damaged seal)
7. Kneeling Worshipper with Goat and Tree-God

8a. Kneeling Worshipper with Tree-God

8b. Worshippers Bearing Branches to Tree-Man-God and Goat

9. Kneeling Worshipper with Tree-Man-God
10. Kneeling Worshipper with Tree-Man-God and Goat
11. Tree-Man-God Merged with Sacred Ficus Tree
12. Tree-Man-God Emerging from Sacred Ficus Tree
13. Śiva Figure as Tree-Man-God
14. Hindu Śiva Liṅgam, Gudimallam, 5 feet high (First Century B.C.E.)
15. Hindu Origin of the Liṅgam (Thirteenth Century)

* * * * *

Mohenjodaro Photographs 1-13, Courtesy Arthur Probsthain and the Archeological Survey of India, Copyright Government of India.

Photograph 14, Ananda K. Coomaraswamy, *History of Indian and Indonesian Art* (New York: Dover Publications, Inc., 1965/1927).

Photograph 15, Musée Guimet, Paris.

Notes

1. The literature on Gandhi and satyagraha is vast. See "Some Suggestions for Further Reading" at the conclusion to this volume.

2. M. K. Gandhi, *Hindu Dharma* (Ahmedabad: Navajivan Publishing House, 1950), p. 404. Italics added.

3. Quoted in T. M. P. Mahadevan, *Ramana Maharshi, The Sage of Arunacala* (London: George Allen & Unwin, Ltd., 1977), p. 17. I have borrowed heavily from Mahadevan's excellent book on Maharshi.

4. Ibid., p. 18.

5. Ibid., pp. 11-12, 18-19. Again, I follow T. M. P. Mahadevan closely in this entire recounting.

6. Ibid., p. 48.

7. Ibid., p. 61.

8. Ibid., p. 62.

9. Ibid.

10. Ibid.

11. C. G. Jung, "The Holy Men of India" in *Psychology and Religion: West and East,* vol. 11 of *The Collected Works of C. G. Jung,* trans. R.F.C. Hull (New York: Pantheon Books, 1958), p. 579. Quoted in Robert A. McDermott and V. S. Naravane, eds., *The Spirit of Modern India* (New York: Thomas Y. Crowell Co., 1974), p. 197. See also Harold Coward, *Jung and Eastern Thought* (Albany: State University of New York Press, 1985) for more on Jung's thoughts on Maharshi and on Jung's "love-hate relationship with India," in general.

12. MacDermott and Naravane, *Spirit of Modern India,* p. 199.

13. *Maharshi's Gospel* (Tiruvannamalai: Sri Ramanasramam, 1949), pp. 30, 33-34. Italics added.

14. Martin Luther King, Jr., *Christian Century* 77 (April 13, 1960), quoted in A. L. Herman, *The Ways of Philosophy: Searching for a Worthwhile Life* (Atlanta: Scholars Press, 1990), chapter 11, "The Way of Christian Satyagraha," p. 258.

15. Thomas Merton, *Zen and the Birds of Appetite* (New York: A New Directions Book, 1968), p. 9.

16. Satsvarupa dasa Goswami, *Śrīla Prabhupāda-līlāmṛta, A Biography of His Divine Grace A.C. Bhaktivedanta Swami Prabhupāda,* 6 vols. (Los Angeles: The Bhaktivedanta Book Trust, 1980-1983), volume I, p. 9.

17. See Troy Wilson Organ, *Hinduism: Its Historical Development* (Woodbury, N.Y.: Barron's Educational Series, Inc., 1974), pp. 147-163.

18. Wendy Doniger O'Flaherty, *Hindu Myths, A Sourcebook Translated From the Sanskrit* (Baltimore: Penguin Books, 1975), p. 217.

19. Ibid.

20. Ibid., p. 218.

21. Ibid., pp. 230-231.

22. Surendranath Dasgupta, *A History of Indian Philosophy,* 5 vols. (Cambridge at the University Press, 1922-1955), vol. 4, p. 392.

23. Ibid., p. 392.

24. Satsvarupa dasa Goswami, *Biography,* vol. 3, p. xix.

25. Ibid., vol. 4, p. xviii.

26. See Organ, *Hinduism, Its Historical Development,* p. 146; A. L. Basham, *The Wonder That Was India* (New York: Grove Press, Inc., 1959), pp. 306-307.

27. Robert S. Ellwood, Jr., *Religious and Spiritual Groups in Modern America* (Englewood Cliffs, N.J.: Prentice-Hall, Inc., 1973), p. 241. See Ellwood's entire discussion of ISKCON, pp. 239-245.

28. Ibid., p. 242.

29. For a discussion of the four noble truths, their origin, and meaning, see A. L. Herman, *An Introduction to Buddhist Thought, A Philosophic History of Indian Buddhism* (Washington, D.C.: University Press of America, 1984), pp. 56-66.

30. Stuart Piggott, *Prehistoric India to 1000 B.C.* (Baltimore: Penguin Books, 1952), p. 14.

31. Walter A. Fairservis, Jr., *The Roots of Ancient India,* 2d ed. rev. (Chicago: University of Chicago Press, 1975), pp. 242, 305.

32. A. D. Pusalker, "The Indus Valley Civilization," in R. C. Mujamdar, ed., *The Vedic Age* (Bombay: Bharatiya Vidya Bhavan, 1951), p. 176.

33. Sir John Marshall, ed., *Mohenjo-daro and the Indus Civilization,* 3 vols. (London: Arthur Probsthain, 1931), vol. 1, p. 15.

34. Ibid., vol. 1, p. 286.

35. J. Gonda observes: "Generally speaking and barring geographical differences the main fig trees are assigned to different gods. The big *pipal, aśvattha* or *ficus religiosa,* is, for instance, in Gujarat, often seen as a shrine of Śiva and believed to be the abode of snakes, the god's pets. . . . This tree [in modern India] is supposed to represent fertility, to give children, and to avert disasters . . ." (J. Gonda, *Viṣṇuism and Śivaism, A Comparison* [London: University of London, 1970], pp. 112-113).

36. S. R. Rao, *Lothal and the Indus Civilization* (New York: Asia Publishing House, 1973), p. 136. See also Ernest J.H. Mackay, *Chanhu-daro Excavations 1935-36* (New Haven, Conn.: American Oriental Society, 1943), pp. 93, 149-150, for a complementary discussion of the sacred trees and leaves depicted on Indus pots and sherds.

37. Several scholars would seem to agree: "Indus religious interests seem, in summary, to have revolved around the *worship* of male animals raised to sacred status, the parallel *worship* of a horned male figure represented as Lord of (male) creatures, *worship* of the lingam as the supreme symbol of male powers, and a conservative emphasis on order, restraint, and purification by bathing. *Worship* of the female powers of fertility and fecundity may have constituted a subsidiary cult at the popular or domestic level" (Thomas J. Hopkins, *The Hindu Religious Tradition* [Encino, Calif.: Dickenson Publishing Company, 1971], p. 9. Emphasis added.

And Mircea Eliade comments: "We shall only point out that the essential mark of Hinduism, the devotional cult, *pūjā,* is a Dravidian contribution. The term *pūjā* itself may be of Dravidian origin. . . . As for mystical devotion, *bhakti,* it is certainly aboriginal in structure, either Dravidian or pre-Dravidian, [Harappān?] . . . (Mircea Eliade, *Yoga, Immortality and Freedom* [Princeton University Press, 1971], p. 348). But see Eliade's specific claims and further evidence for the pre-Dravidian and Harappān origins of bhakti activity on pp. 353-358.

See also A. L. Basham, *The Wonder That Was India,* pp. 22-24, who speaks to the same matters regarding the worship of those objects depicted on the seals. See also David R. Kinsley, *Hinduism, A Cultural Perspective* (Prentice-Hall, Inc., 1982), p. 10, and R. C. Zaehner, *Hinduism* (Oxford University Press, 1972), p. 16, both of whom trace "worship" back to the Indus civilization.

But several scholars would seem to disagree. See C. V. Narayana Ayyar, *Origin and Early History of Śaivism in South India* (Madras: University of Madras, 1974) where it is argued that Śaivism has its origin in the God Rudra of the *Vedas*. And see A. L. Basham who, in his final work, changed his mind on the entire matter of the origin of the Hindu Lord Śiva from this ithyphallic, tiger-masked image from the Indus Valley: "In fact the evidence for any kind of continuity between this prehistoric god and Śiva is rather weak." *The Origins and Development of Classical Hinduism* (Boston: Beacon Press, 1989), p. 4. Finally, see Doris Srinivasan, "Unhinging Siva from the Indus Civilization," *Journal of the Royal Asiatic Society of Great Britain and Ireland*, 1984, no. 1, pp. 77-89.

38. Marshall, *Mohenjo-daro,* vol. 1, p. 285.

39. Pulsaker, "Indus Valley Civilization," p. 200.

40. Ibid.

41. Ibid.

42. Ibid.

43. George F. Dales, "The Decline of the Harappans," *Scientific American,* vol. 214, no. 5 (1966), p. 95.

44. See *Ṛg Veda* VI. 27.5 for a reference to the city of "Hariyūpīyā." The hymn is dedicated to Indra, the Āryan God of War.

45. *Ṛg Veda* X. 89.7.

46. *Ṛg Veda* II. 20.7.

47. *Ṛg Veda* VII. 21.5.

48. Dales, "The Decline of the Harappans," pp. 95-96.

49. Sir Mortimer Wheeler, *Civilizations of the Indus Valley and Beyond* (New York: McGraw-Hill, 1966), p. 75.

50. Ibid., p. 76. Walter Fairservis also comments: "At Mohenjodaro the Mature occupation deteriorates in the Late Harappan to the destruction or covering over of the fine buildings of the earlier period with hundreds of miserable huts; refuse and brickbats choked the streets and the grand avenues; the "citadel" itself was surmounted by poor habitations much as were ancient Rome, modern Boston, London and New York. Here was certainly a breakdown of dharma" (Fairservis, *The Roots of Ancient India,* p. 302-303).

51. But that was not the end. S. R. Rao states: "It is now generally agreed that the Indus Civilization did not die a sudden death with the destruction of Harappā and Mohenjodaro in ca. 1900 B.C., but survived for three centuries more outside the Indus Valley" (Gregory L. Possehl, ed., *Harappān Civilization, A Contemporary Perspective* [Warminster, England: Aris & Phillips, Ltd., 1982], p. 354).

52. See Mircea Eliade, *Yoga, Immortality and Freedom,* pp. 354-355. Eliade quotes with approval Stuart Piggott's conclusion (*Prehistoric India,* [Pelican, 1950], p. 203) regarding the Harappān influence on Hinduism: "It is even possible that early historic Hindu society owed more to Harappā than it did to the Sanskrit-speaking invaders." p. 356.

53. *Atharva-Veda* VI.138 in *Hymns of the Atharva-Veda,* trans. Maurice Bloomfield (New York: Greenwood Press, Publisher, 1969 [orig. published 1897]), pp. 108-109.

54. *Ṛg Veda* III. 62.10. All quotations from the *Ṛg Veda* are based on the translation of Ralph T.V. Griffith in *The Hymns of the Ṛg Veda* (Delhi: Motilal Banarsidass, 1973 [orig. published 1896]).

55. *Ṛg Veda* X. 90.11-12.

56. *Ṛg Veda* X. 121.1-10, after Griffith with some minor changes that make the choral chanting of this ecological hymn a truly moving experience.

57. *Ṛg Veda* VII. 89.1-5.

58. *Ṛg Veda* X. 89.10.

59. *Ṛg Veda* I. 154.5, 6.

60. *Ṛg Veda* VII. 86.1-8.

61. See Frits Staal, "What is Happening in Classical Indology? - A Review Article," *The Journal of Asian Studies,* vol. 41, no. 2 (1982), p. 279.

62. *Ṛg Veda* IV. 23.8-10.

63. *Rg Veda* II. 28.7-9.

64. Franklin Edgerton, *The Bhagavad Gītā* (New York: Harper Torchbooks, 1964), p. 111.

65. Ibid., p. 116.

66. Ibid. This was one of the central themes of the *Brāhmaṇas:* Knowledge was essential to the proper working of the sacrifice and to the securing of the desired benefit; no knowledge, no result. Without knowledge, the ritual sacrifice was "no better than an offering poured on dead ashes," as a later text stated. See Thomas J. Hopkins's excellent summary, *The Hindu Religious Tradition,* pp. 31-35.

67. *Chāndogya Upaniṣad* IV. 4.1-5. Author's translation of the *Upaniṣads.*

68. *Chāndogya Upaniṣad,* VI. 10.1-3.

69. *Chāndogya Upaniṣad* VI. 13.1-3.

70. The concept of saṁsāra, the argument states, does not occur in the *Vedas,* but it is present in the *Upaniṣads.* So where did it come from? One answer, and one that seems to have fairly strong support, is that it, like bhakti yoga previously, came from the Harappāns of the Indus Valley civilization. See Notes 37 and 52 above.

71. *Bṛhadāraṇyaka Upaniṣad,* VI. 2.2.

72. See "The Guiding Principle or Person" above; see also the scholarly attention that has been shown to the law of karma and its origins in Wendy Doniger O'Flaherty. ed., *Karma and Rebirth in Classical Indian Traditions* (University of California Press, 1980). See also the fine collection of papers in S. S. Rama Rao Pappu, ed., *The Dimensions of Karma* (Delhi: Chanakya Publications, 1987).

73. *Bṛhadāraṇyaka Upaniṣad* III. 2.13.

74. *Śvetāśvatara Upaniṣad* V. 11-12. Emphasis added.

75. *Muṇḍaka Upaniṣad* III. 2.2.

76. *Muṇḍaka Upaniṣad* I. 2.5-10.

77. I first heard the story at Harvard in 1962.

78. *Laws of Manu* II. 173, 176-177, translated by G. Buhler, *Sacred Books of the East,* vol. 25 (Oxford: Clarendon Press, 1975 [orig. published 1886]).

79. Ibid., VI. 3-4, 29.

80. Ibid., VI. 36, 41-43.

81. See *Chāndogya Upaniṣad* VIII. 7-12 for a discussion of the final blissful state that lies beyond annihilation and nothingness. I say "central thrust" for as with all things Indian and Hindu there is disagreement about the nature of the prescription for liberation from suffering for the *Upaniṣads.* This disagreement amongst the great philosophers of India's past and present centers around both the metaphysics and the epistemology of the *Upaniṣads.* There are at least as many interpretations of the *Upaniṣads* as there are of the *Gītā,* as many Gandhis, Maharshis, and Bhaktivedantas standing by with their interpretations of the former as there are with the latter. By

"central thrust" here, I mean essentially the kind of interpretation of the *Upaniṣads* that Ramana Maharshi would give to it, wherein its metaphysics is a transcendental monism and its epistemology is a mystical intuitionism: In short, this "central thrust" is that of advaita (nondualistic) Vedānta and follows the traditional interpretation given by the Indian advaitin, Śaṁkarācarya (788-820 C.E.).

82. *The Laws of Manu*, III. 56-57.

83. Ibid., III. 58-59.

84. Ibid., IX. 2-3.

85. Ibid., V. 151.

86. Ibid., V. 154-155.

87. Ibid., V. 156-157.

88. To aid those ponderings the reader might consult the following extremely interesting works: Rita M. Gross, ed., *Beyond Androcentrism: New Essays on Women and Religion* (Atlanta, Ga.: Scholars Press, 1981); and Nancy A. Falk and Rita M. Gross, eds., *Unspoken Worlds: Women's Religious Lives*, (Belmont, Calif.: Wadsworth Publishing Co., 1989); and especially Katherine Young, "Hinduism," in Arvind Sharma, ed., *Women in World Religions*, (Albany: State University of New York Press, 1987), pp. 59-103. See also the very fine study by Harold Coward, Julius Lipner, and Katherine Young, *Hindu Ethics: Purity, Abortion, and Euthanasia* (Albany: State University of New York Press, 1989). Coward's chapter, "Purity in Hinduism," provides a good explanation of Manu's attitude towards women in a discussion of the male society's fear of menstrual pollution. Coward's history of the evolution of the Hindu attitude toward women is superb. Similarly, Lipner's chapter, "The Classical Hindu View on Abortion and the Moral Status of the Unborn," offers an insightful presentation on the status of women in Hindu society with a fine discussion of a woman's individual rights versus the rights of the community in the matter of abortion.

89. *Maitrī Upaniṣad* III. 5. For more on the guṇas, see Chapter 3, "Guṇas, Varṇas, and Yogas."

90. *Muṇḍaka Upaniṣad* II. 2.3-4.

91. *Śvetāśvatara Upaniṣad* I. 13-14. See also *S.U.* II. 8-10 for a description of the way meditation should be practiced.

92. *Maitrī Upaniṣad* VI. 18.

93. *Maitrī Upaniṣad* VI. 29.

94. For a fascinating contemporary discussion of the relation between samādhi as a mental state and samādhi as final liberation, see the distinction between "samādhi with support" and "samādhi without support" in Mircea Eliade, *Yoga, Immortality and Freedom*, pp. 76-100.

95. *Bhagavad Gītā* I. 27-31. Author's translation of the *Bhagavad Gītā*, hereafter referred to as *B.G.* The translations rely heavily on A. L. Herman, *The Bhagavad Gītā, A Translation and Critical Commentary* (Springfield, Ill.: Charles C. Thomas Publishers, 1973).

96. *B.G.* I. 43-47.

97. *B.G.* II. 11-12.

98. *B.G.* II. 13.

99. *B.G.* II. 16-18.

100. *B.G.* II. 19-22.

101. *B.G.* II. 30.

102. *B.G.* III. 2.

103. *B.G.* II. 31.

104. *B.G.* II. 32.

105. *B.G.* II. 33.

106. *B.G.* II. 34-36.

107. *B.G.* II. 37.

108. *B.G.* II. 39.

109. *B.G.* II. 43, 45-56.

110. *B.G.* II. 47-51.

111. *B.G.* II. 55-57. See also *B.G.* V. 16-23, VI. 18-32, XII. 13-20, XIV. 22-27, XVI. 1-3 and XVIII. 49-54 for further descriptions of this jīvanmukta.

112. *B.G.* II. 60.

113. *B.G.* II. 62-63.

114. *B.G.* II. 64-65.

115. *B.G.* II. 61. Emphasis added.

116. *B.G.* IV. 5-8.

117. *B.G.* IX. 31-32.

118. *B.G.* IX. 33-34.

119. *B.G.* XVIII. 55.

120. *B.G.* XVIII. 64-66, 57-58.

121. *B.G.* V. 27-28.

122. *B.G.* VI. 10-15.

123. *B.G.* V. 16-17.

124. *B.G.* XII. 8-12.

125. *B.G.* XIII. 24.

126. *B.G.* XVIII. 72-73.

127. *B.G.* II. 36.

128. *B.G.* II. 56.

129. *B.G.* V. 22.

130. *B.G.* VIII. 15.

131. *B.G.* VI. 23.

132. *B.G.* VI. 32.

133. *B.G.* VI. 17.

134. *B.G.* VI. 23.

135. *B.G.* III. 37, 39, 43.

136. *B.G.* XVI. 21.

137. *B.G.* V. 16. See also *B.G.* XIII. 11; XIV. 16, 17; XVI. 4.

138. *B.G.* XVIII. 65.

139. *B.G.* V. 17.

140. Karma yoga may actually have originated in the *Vedas*. Frits Staal observed: "In the *Bhagavad Gītā, tyāga* ["the formula pronounced by the Yajamāna [a priest in the Vedic ritual] at the time of the oblation by which he renounces the benefits or fruits of the ritual in favor of the deity...are of the form: This is for Agni, not for me."] means abandoning and renouncing the fruits of all activity, and is advocated as the highest goal of life." Quoted in O'Flaherty, *Karma and Rebirth in Classical Indian Traditions,* p. 12.

141. See Table 2.3 above, p. 85.

142. *Republic* 441c, d, in *The Dialogues of Plato,* translated by B. Jowett, 2 vols., (New York: Random House, 1937), vol. 1, p. 705.

143. Ibid., 441d, e.

144. Ibid., 473d, p. 757.

145. For more on Plato's way to liberation from suffering see A. L. Herman, *The Ways of Philosophy,* chapter 4, "The Way of Justice." Strictly speaking, Plato seems to have reserved his educational plan just for the guardians, the two highest classes. These Platonic dvijas kept the masses at bay and thereby ensured happiness for all.

146. Wendy Doniger O'Flaherty, *The Origins of Evil in Hindu Mythology* (Los Angeles: University of California Press, 1976), p. 16.

147. *B.G.* XVIII. 58.

148. *B.G.* XVIII. 62.

149. *B.G.* XVIII. 66.

150. Mahadev Desai, *The Gita According to Gandhi* (Ahmedabad: Navajivan Publishing House, 1946), pp. 127-130, 130-131, 132-133, 134.

151. *The Collected Works of Ramana Maharshi,* ed. and annot. Arthur Osborne (London: Rider & Company, 1959), pp. 101-104.

152. A. C. Bhaktivedanta Swami Prabhupada, *Bhagavad-gītā As It Is,* complete edition (London: Collier-Macmillan Ltd., 1972), pp. ii, xiii.

153. Ibid., p. xii.

154. Ibid.

155. Ibid., p. 26.

156. Ibid., p. 870.

157. Ibid., p. 871.

158. Ibid., pp. 359, 360.

159. Ibid., p. 359.

160. Ibid., p. 134. *B.G.* 2.49.

161. *B.G.* II. 49 in Desai, *The Gita According to Gandhi*, p. 162.

162. *B.G.* II. 50. in Desai, *The Gita According to Gandhi*, p. 163.

163. *B.G.* 2.50 in Bhaktivedanta, *The Bhagavad-gītā As It Is*, p. 135.

164. *B.G.* V. 16-17. Author's translation.

165. Bhaktivedanta, *The Bhagavad-gītā As It Is*, p. 291.

166. *B.G.* 10.12 in Bhaktivedanta, *The Bhagavad-gītā As It Is*, p. 5. This verse and those that follow come from the Introduction to Bhaktivedanta's translation of the *Gita*. I take them in the order in which he gives them.

167. *B.G.* 8.5 in Bhaktivedanta, *The Bhagavad-gītā As It Is*, p. 22.

168. *B.G.* 8.7 in Bhaktivedanta, *The Bhagavad-gītā As It Is*, p. 24.

169. *B.G.* 6.47 in Bhaktivedanta, *The Bhagavad-gītā As It Is*, p. 26.

170. *B.G.* 8.8 in Bhaktivedanta, *The Bhagavad-gītā As It Is*, p. 26.

171. *B.G.* 9.32-33 in Bhaktivedanta, *The Bhagavad-gītā As It Is*, p. 27.

172. *B.G.* 18.66 in Bhaktivedanta, *The Bhagavad-gītā As It Is*, p. 28.

173. Ibid.

Some Suggestions for Further Reading

This brief bibliography lists only a few of the many fine books by and about Hindus. It includes books that the student of Indian philosophy and religion might find useful for extending and deepening an already awakened curiousity about matters Hindulogical.

Ancient India and The Indus Valley Civilization

Walter A. Fairservis, Jr., *The Roots of Ancient India,* 2d ed. rev., (Chicago: University of Chicago Press, 1975). Undoubtedly one of the best studies of the Indus Valley civilization, its origins and complexities, and destruction.

Stuart Piggott, *Prehistoric India* (Baltimore: Penguin Books, 1952). Piggott's book remains one of the classic expositions of archaeological India. It is well informed, well written, and makes exciting reading about a little-known period in man's ancient past. Required reading for all serious students of Indian thought.

Gregory L. Possehl, ed., *Harappān Civilization, A Contemporary Perspective,* (Warminster, England: Aris & Phillips, Ltd., 1982). A collection of very good essays on the most recent research on the Indus culture with some new speculations on the demise of the Indus civilization.

Sir Mortimer Wheeler, *Civilizations of the Indus Valley and Beyond* (New York: McGraw-Hill Book Company, 1972). A brief, exciting, colorful account of the Indus Valley culture by one of the greatest on-site archaeologists of the twentieth century.

The Vedas and the Upaniṣads

Franklin Edgerton, *The Beginnings of Indian Philosophy* (Cambridge: Harvard University Press, 1970). Fine translations of Vedic and Upaniṣadic texts with selections from the *Gītā* and the *Mahâbhārata* make this an exceptional collection of first-rate materials.

Arthur Berriedale Keith, *The Religion and Philosophy of the Veda and Upanishads,* 2 vols. (Delhi: Motilal Banarsidass, 1970/1925). Despite its age it remains the classic text on its subject. Required reading for all serious students of Indian thought.

Wendy Doniger O'Flaherty, trans., *The Rig Veda,* (Baltimore: Penguin Books, 1982). A grand translation of 108 hymns into an English that everyone can understand.

That, together with the copious notes and an informative and entertaining commentary, make this a really superlative text.

Raimundo Panikker, *The Vedic Experience: Mantramanjari* (Los Angeles: University of California Press, 1977). A superior set of translations and commentaries from the *Vedas, Brāhmaṇas,* and *Upaniṣads* with excellent introductions explaining the meaning and continuing significance of these great works.

The Bhagavad Gītā

Swami Prabhavananda and Christopher Isherwood, *The Bhagavad Gita: The Song of God* (Los Angeles: Vedanta Press, 1987/1944). A moving and poetic rendering of the Sanskrit makes this a joy to read, but the translation, while beautiful, is not as faithful to the original as one might have wished.

S. Radhakrishnan, *The Bhagavad Gītā* (New York: Harper Colophon Books, 1973/1948). Decent translation with a brilliant introductory essay and a running commentary on almost every one of the 700 verses. A faithful but not altogether beautiful translation.

David White, *The Bhagavad Gītā, A New Translation with Commentary* (New York: Peter Lang, 1988). This new work is a teacher's dream. The commentary sparkles with insights and wisdom that other commentaries do not have, and the translation is both faithful and beautiful.

Mohandas K. Gandhi

Margaret Chatterjee, *Gandhi's Religious Thought* (Notre Dame, Ind.: University of Notre Dame Press, 1986). A fine recounting of Gandhi's way of satyagraha by a fine scholar.

Louis Fischer, *The Life of Mahatma Gandhi* (New York: Harper and Row, 1983). Probably the best complete biography of Gandhi's life and times by a non-Indian.

Mohandas K. Gandhi, *An Autobiography* or *The Story of My Experiments With Truth* (Ahmedabad: Navajivan Publishing House, 1940/1927). Written by Gandhi in and out of prison in 1924 and 1925, *The Story of My Experiments With Truth* was produced for publication serially in Gandhi's paper, *Young India.* Each chapter forms an episode in his life and each ends by expounding a moral truth.

M. K. Gandhi, *Hindu Dharma* (Ahmedabad: Navajivan Publishing House, 1950). Insightful brief selections form Gandhi's newspapers, *Young India* and *Harijan,* that relate to Hinduism and the duty ("dharma") of Hindus within that religion ("dharma," again). The pieces range from fasting, the *Gītā,* and nonviolence, to cow protection, untouchables, widowhood, and women. A fascinating collection.

Ramana Bhagavan Maharshi

T.M.P. Mahadevan, *Ramana Maharshi, The Sage of Arunacala* (London: George Allen & Unwin, Ltd., 1977). This is a moving and factual account of one of the world's greatest mystics and his impact on Hinduism, composed by a devoted disciple and now-famous Indian philosopher.

Maharshi's Gospel (Books I and II) (Tiruvannamalai: Sri Ramanasramam, 1949). A small book with the Master speaking to his disciples and followers on such topics as work and renunciation, silence and solitude, the guru and his grace, and Self-realization.

Arthur Osborne, ed., *The Collected Works of Ramana Maharshi* (London: Rider & Company, 1959). The editor has done a fine job assembling and editing this collection of Maharshi's wisdom. It is undoubtedly the best introduction to the great Master through the great Master available in English.

Swami A.C. Bhaktivedanta

A. C. Bhaktivedanta Swami Prabhupada, *Śrī Caitanya Caritāmṛta* (Los Angeles: The Bhaktivedanta Book Trust, 1974). Bhaktivedanta's translation from the Bengali of the teachings of Lord Caitanya together with the Swami's notes and commentaries in several volumes. It is devotional reading at its best.

Satsvarupadasa Goswami, *Śrīla Prabhupāda-līlāmṛta, A Biography of His Divine Grace A.C. Bhaktivedanta Swami Prabhupāda*, 6 vols. (Los Angeles: The Bhaktivedanta Book Trust, 1980-1983). The life and times of A. C. Bhaktivedanta written with wit, charm, and devotion by a loving disciple.

Hinduism in General

A. L. Basham, *The Wonder That Was India* (New York: Grove Press, Inc., 1959). It is probably still the best history of the culture surrounding developing Hinduism up until 1200 C.E. Required reading for all serious students of Indian thought.

A. L. Basham, ed., *A Cultural History of India* (Oxford: Clarendon Press, 1975). Basham's last great work with some grand selections and commentaries.

Klaus Klostermaier, *A Survey of Hinduism* (Albany: State University Press of New York, 1989). A really grand and broad view of Hinduism by a first-rate scholar.

John M. Koller, *The Indian Way* (New York: Macmillan and Co., 1987). An excellent introduction to Indian philosophies and religions written by a grand scholar and teacher who writes clearly and well.

John M. and Patricia Koller, eds., *A Sourcebook in Asian Philosophy* (Macmillan Publishing Company, Inc., 1991). A fine collection from not only Hindu, Jain, and Buddhist works but other Asian philosophic and religious texts as well.

Wendy Doniger O'Flaherty, trans., *Hindu Myths,* (Baltimore: Penguin Books, 1975). Seventy-five stories of Hindu Gods and demons taken from the classical Indian philosophic and religious texts, beautifully rendered into a readable and charming translation by a great scholar.

Wendy Doniger O'Flaherty, ed. and trans., *Textual Sources for the Study of Hinduism* (Chicago: University of Chicago Press, 1990). An exceptional gathering of basic Hindu materials translated from the fundamental Hindu texts by a first-rate Hindologist.

Index-Glossary

Absorption into *Brahman*, 24, 32, 34, 78, 86, 118, 119, 121, 130
Act (a happening or activity), 103-105
Action (an event consisting of Motive, Act and Consequences), 102, 103-105, 119, 120
advaita Vedānta (a non-dualistic metaphysical view of the *Upaniṣads*), 15, 157-158
Agni (the Vedic Lord of fire), 51
Ahmedabad, 4, 5
ajñāna ("ignorance"), 116, 118, 130
Altruism (a concern or caring only for the interests of others), 12
Anxiety,48, 61, 134
aparā Brahman, see Brahman
Āpas (the Vedic Lord of the waters),52
Āraṇyakas (the *śruti* "forest texts" for qualified renunciates; arranged sometime between 800-600 B.C.E.), 50
Argument (any reasoning designed to prove or disprove a proposition), 92
  Duty-calls argument, 98-99
  Four brahminical arguments, 98-100
  Heaven-can-be-yours argument, 99
  Live forever argument, 95-96
  Metaphysical priorities argument, 96-98
  Shame-will-be-yours argument, 99
  Sin-will-be-yours argument, 99
  Two Brahmanical arguments, 95-98, 100
Aristotle (Greek philosopher, 384-322 B.C.E.), 65
Arjuna (the Pandava human hero of the *Bhagavad Gītā* (*see also Mahābhārata*), 23, 90-142 *passim*, 147
Arjuna's dilemma, *see* Dilemma
Arjuna problem, the, 114-115
Arjuna's problems, 92-94, 100, 105
artha ("wealth"), 78
arthas ("aims or goals" of life) (*see also artha, dharma, kāma, mokṣa*), 75, 77-78
Āryans ("the noble ones;" the nomadic warrior-invaders of India of the second millennium B.C.E.), 20, 29, 37, 38, 44, 45, 47, 49, 50, 51, 53, 70, 98
āśrama (a communal retreat or place of retirement), 4
āśramas ("stages" of life), 75-77, 78, 81
  brahmacarya āśrama (student stage), 76, 77
  gṛhastha āśrama (householder stage), 76, 77
  sannyāsa āśrama (ascetic wanderer stage), 2, 9, 19, 77
  vānaprastha āśrama (forest dweller stage), 76-77
Atharva Veda, see Vedas
Atheism (the view that there are no Gods), 19, 61-62
Ātman (the impersonal Self, Spirit or *Brahman* within each person) (*see also Brahman*, Self), 14, 67, 68, 69,

Action, dilemma of, 100, 101, 106, 107, 120, 131
Arjuna's dilemma, 115, 131
Family dilemma, 94, 97, 98, 100
God-karma dilemma, 129, 130
Personal dilemma, 95, 96, 97, 98, 99, 100, 101, 120
Savior dilemma, 110-111

Dravidians, 155

duḥkha (anxiety, stress, frustration, inadequacy), 30, 115, 118, 119, 130

Duty-calls argument, the, *see* Argument

dvija (the twice-born, i.e., the ritually born-again, *brahmins, kṣatriyas* and *vaiśyas* but not *śūdras*) (*see also varṇa dharma*), 76, 82, 85

Eckhart, Meister Johannes (German theologian and religious mystic, 1260-1327), 16

Edgerton, Franklin, 62, 157, 163

Eliade, Mircea, 155, 156, 158

Ellwood, Robert S., Jr., 154

Ethics (the investigation into the problems of right and wrong in human conduct) (*see also karma yoga*, satyagraha), 3-4, 7-8, 14-15, 16, 25-26

Extraordinary Brahmanism, 61-62, 63

Fairservis, Walter A., Jr., 154, 156, 163

Falk, Nancy A., 158

Family dilemma, the, *see* Dilemma

Fischer, Louis, 164

Forgiveness of sins, 56-58, 128-129

Four Noble Truths, the, 30

Francis, Saint, of Assisi (Italian monk and preacher, 1182-1226), 15

Fundamentalist Kṛṣṇaism, 27-28

Gandhi, Mohandas Karamchand (Hindu statesman and follower of the way of brahminism, 1869-1948), 1-8, 9, 12, 15-16, 24, 31, 32-35, 65, 87, 130, 131-134, 137, 138, 140, 142, 145, 147, 153, 164-165

Gautama the Buddha (the "awakened one" and founder of Buddhism, 563-483 B.C.E.), 27, 30

Glaucon (Plato's brother, fifth century B.C.E.), 125, 126

God(s), 3, 4, 7-8, 10, 11, 13, 14, 15, 16, 17, 19, 20, 22, 23, 24, 25, 32, 33, 34, 35, 36, 42, 43, 45, 48, 49, 50, 51-52, 53-56, 57, 58, 60, 61, 62, 64, 72, 78, 79, 91, 92, 107-110, 117, 119, 120, 128, 129-130, 131, 132, 133, 134, 146

Goddess(es), 32

God-karma dilemma, the, *see* Dilemma

Gonda, J., 154

Goswami, Satsvarupa dasa, 153, 154, 165

Grace (the "favor" of God), 110, 128-129

Great Mother, the, 49

Great Salt March, the, 4-6

gṛhya sacrifices, 58

Griffith, Ralph T. V., 156

Gross, Rita, 158

guṇa-nature (the character of an entity as caused by its inherent *guṇas*),

guṇas ("ligaments," "strings"; the three strands or qualities from which all existing and created entities are woven or composed), 81-83, 85, 102, 121, 122, 148

About the Book and Author

In this lucid and incisive account of Hinduism, A. L. Herman introduces the reader to one of the great belief systems of our time. Professor Herman begins with the assumption that philosophies and religions exist primarily to cope with human problems, and he demonstrates that a valuable way of approaching Hinduism is to ask what problems it seeks to solve and how it goes about solving them.

Herman identifies three distinct traditions and treats both their historical roots --as far back as 2500 B.C.E.--and their twentieth-century manifestations as seen in three representative figures.

These figures--Mohandas Gandhi, Ramana Maharshi, and A. C. Bhaktivedanta --were united in their concern for human suffering, but they had different understandings of the human predicament and offered very different solutions for it. Herman shows how these differences are neatly brought out by their distinctive readings of the classic Hindu texts: the *Vedas*, *Upanisads*, and, especially, the *Bhagavad Gītā*.

Herman's introduction is bold, original, and iconoclastic. It is also enlightening and thought provoking and provides an important reading of the philosophical and historical aspects of this great tradition. Scholars and their students will be grateful for this accessible entree to Hindu thought.

A. L. Herman is professor of philosophy at the University of Wisconsin-Stevens Point. Educated at Stanford, Harvard, and the University of Minnesota, he is the author of *India Folk Tales* (1968); *The Bhagavad Gītā, A Translation and Critical Commentary* (1973); *An Introduction to Indian Thought* (1976); *An Introduction to Buddhist Thought* (1984); *The Problem of Evil and Indian Thought*, Second Edition (1990); *The Ways of Philosophy* (1990); and coeditor with R. T. Blackwood of *Problems in Philosophy: West and East* (1975).